1997.

HORS D'OEUVRES

HORS D'OEUVRES

JUNE BUDGEN

Photography by
PER ERICSON

PUBLISHED BY
SALAMANDER BOOKS LIMITED
LONDON

Published 1986 by Salamander Books Ltd.,
129–137 York Way, London N7 9LG
By arrangement with Merehurst Fairfax,
51–57 Lacy Road, London SW15 1RP
© Merehurst Fairfax and June Budgen 1986

10 9 8 7 6 5 4

ISBN: 0 86101 238 0

Editors: Susan Tomnay, Beverly Le Blanc, Chris Fayers
Designers: Susan Kinealy, Roger Daniels, Richard Slater, Stuart Willard
Food stylist: June Budgen
Photographer: Per Ericson
Typeset by Lineage
Colour separation by Fotographics Ltd, London–Hong Kong
Printed and bound in Spain by Bookprint, S.L.
The publishers would like to thank Dansabb for supplying Sasaki Crystal.

CONTENTS

INTRODUCTION

It is customary to serve hors d'oeuvres as a start to a luncheon or dinner or for nibbling at a drinks party, but they can also be combined to make a complete meal.

For a formal dinner, choose an hors d'oeuvre that is light but piquant so it will enhance the meal that is to follow. When an hors d'oeuvre is served before a salad or a light main course, a more substantial dish, such as an individual quiche, would be more appropriate.

Hors d'oeuvres for a drinks party should be 'finger food' that can be picked up and eaten with one hand. These parties require a great deal of preparation and I suggest choosing some of the dishes that can be cooked ahead of time and frozen, ready to reheat just before serving. Some hors d'oeuvres which freeze well are small quiches, meatballs, pizzas, yeast rolls and filo pastries. Don't forget – if some of the finger food is a bit messy to eat, provide lots of small napkins.

You don't have to be a Cordon Bleu chef to produce a spectacular meal consisting of all hors d'oeuvres, and a meal like this is especially suited to picnics where guests nibble all day. I am not allowed to appear at picnics without my Egg & Caviar Spread, page 91 and yet, like most of the recipes in this book, it is very easy to make.

SPICY FISHBALLS

500 g (1 lb) white fish fillets
1 teaspoon grated fresh root ginger
1½ teaspoons curry powder
1 teaspoon salt
4 spring onions, finely chopped
3 eggs
125 g (4 oz/1 cup) dry breadcrumbs
3 tablespoons sesame seeds
vegetable oil for frying
lemon slices and yogurt, to serve

Poach fish fillets in water until cooked. Allow fish to cool. Flake the fish, removing any bones and skin.

Put the fish into a bowl with the ginger, curry powder, salt and onions. Beat one of the eggs and add to the fish. Mix well with a fork and form the mixture into 24 small balls.

Mix the breadcrumbs with the sesame seeds. Beat the remaining eggs in a shallow dish. Roll the fish balls in the eggs, then in the breadcrumbs. Pour oil to 1 cm (½ inch) depth in a heavy-based frying pan. Heat oil and fry the fishballs until golden. Drain on absorbent paper. Serve warm with lemon slices and, if liked, yogurt for dipping. *Makes 24.*

—— SEAFOOD COCKTAILS ——

selection of cooked prawns, oysters, Pickled
  Squid, page 34, and crabmeat
300 ml (10 fl oz) double (thickened) cream
2 teaspoons horseradish relish
1 tablespoon tomato sauce
2 tablespoons tomato paste
few drops of Tabasco sauce
squeeze of lemon juice
salt and pepper

Peel the prawns and remove the veins.
Cover and chill with the other seafood
until ready to serve.

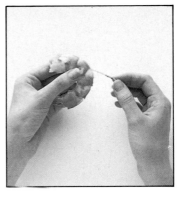

Combine the cream with the
horseradish, tomato sauce, tomato
paste and Tabasco.

Add lemon juice, salt and pepper to
taste. If the sauce is very thin, whisk
lightly. Cover and chill up to 3 days
until ready to serve. Serve with the
prawns, the oysters in their shells and
the crabmeat in chunks. The squid is
sliced. Turn the seafood sauce into a
bowl and surround with the seafood.
Serve immediately. Serves 4 to 6.

— SEAFOOD PÂTÉ —

500 g (1 lb) white fish fillets
500 g (1 lb) raw prawns
90 g (3 oz) butter
6 spring onions, chopped
250 g (8 oz) scallops (optional)
1 clove garlic, crushed
2 tablespoons Cognac or brandy
125 ml (4 fl oz/½ cup) single cream
1 tablespoon lemon juice
1 teaspoon paprika
good pinch of cayenne pepper
lemon slices, fresh dill sprigs and peeled cooked
**   prawns, to serve**

To remove the skin from the fish, place the fish, skin side down and use a sharp knife to separate flesh, pulling skin from side to side. Cut the fish into chunks. Peel and de-vein the prawns.

Melt the butter in a frying pan and gently sauté the spring onions for 2 minutes. Add the fish, prawns, scallops (if used) and garlic. Cook, turning until the prawns turn pink and the fish flakes.

Warm the Cognac, ignite and pour over the fish mixture. When the flames subside, add the cream. Stir in the lemon juice, paprika and cayenne. Cool. Put the mixture into a food processor and blend. Turn the mixture into one large or several small serving dishes, cover and chill until firm. Garnish with lemon slices, sprigs of dill and prawns. Serve with crackers, Melba toast or celery. *Serves 10.*

SEAFOOD TOASTS

2 slices white bread
250 g (8 oz) raw prawns
250 g (8 oz) white fish fillets
2 eggs
1 tablespoon ginger wine or dry sherry
1 tablespoon soy sauce
½ teaspoon salt
1 tablespoon cornflour
fresh parsley sprigs (optional)
vegetable oil for deep-frying

Trim crusts thickly from bread so each square measures about 7 cm (2¾ in). Cut each diagonally into halves.

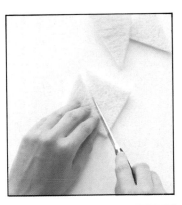

Peel and de-vein the prawns. Remove any bones and skin from the fish. Put prawns and fish into a food processor with 1 egg, the ginger wine, soy sauce, salt and cornflour. Blend to a smooth paste. Spread evenly on the pieces of bread.

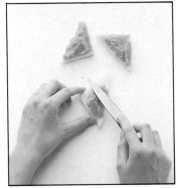

Beat the remaining egg and brush over the spread seafood. Press a sprig of parsley on top of each. Heat the oil in a frying pan. When hot add the seafood-topped bread, a few pieces at a time. Turn triangles occasionally until golden all over. Drain and repeat until all are cooked. Serve hot or warm. *Makes 24.*

ANCHOVY BEIGNETS

60 g (2 oz) butter
125 ml (4 fl oz/½ cup) water
60 g (2 oz/½ cup) plain flour
4 canned anchovy fillets, drained and mashed
2 eggs
30 g (1 oz) slivered almonds
vegetable oil for deep-frying

Cut the butter into cubes and put into a saucepan with the water. Heat until butter melts, then bring to the boil.

Add the flour all at once and stir for about 1 minute, until the paste leaves the side of the saucepan. Cool. Transfer to a bowl. Beat in the anchovy fillets and eggs, 1 at a time, until mixture is glossy. Stir in the slivered almonds.

Heat the oil in a medium saucepan. When hot drop a few teaspoonfuls of the anchovy mixture into the oil. Cook a few at a time for about 5 minutes, until golden. Remove with a slotted spoon and drain on absorbent paper. Repeat until all the batter is used. Serve hot. *Makes 12 to 15.*

- ARTICHOKES WITH CAVIAR -

440 g (14 oz) can artichoke bottoms
3-6 slices white bread
2 tablespoons vegetable oil
2 tablespoons thick sour cream
1 tablespoon Aioli, page 93, or homemade
**   mayonnaise**
juice of ½ lemon
1 tablespoon snipped fresh chives
6 teaspoons black or red caviar

Drain the artichoke bottoms discarding the liquid in the can.

Cut out 6 rounds of bread using a
biscuit cutter. Heat the oil in a shallow
pan. When hot, fry the bread rounds
until golden on both sides. Drain on
absorbent paper. Combine the sour
cream and Aioli, adding a few drops of
lemon juice to taste, then stir in the
snipped chives.

The bread can be prepared 24 hours in
advance and stored in an airtight
container, and the cream can be mixed
and chilled ready to assemble at the last
moment. Place the artichoke bottoms
on the bread rounds, top with a
spoonful of the sour cream mixture
and the caviar. *Makes 6.*

CAVIAR MOUSSE

250 g (8 oz) black caviar
2 teaspoons gelatine
125 ml (4 fl oz/½ cup) boiling water
300 ml (10 fl oz) carton thick sour cream
3 spring onions, finely chopped
hard-boiled eggs and fresh herbs (optional), to
 garnish

The caviar mousse is best not made more than 24 hours before serving. Put the caviar in a bowl. Dissolve the gelatine in the boiling water and stir into the caviar.

Divide the caviar mixture between four small moulds or pour into one large mould. Chill until set. Meanwhile, combine the sour cream with the spring onions. Cover and chill until needed.

Unmould the caviar shapes by dipping the moulds into hot water and turning upside down on to a serving platter. Garnish with cut-out shapes of hard-boiled egg whites, sieved yolks, and sprigs of fresh herbs. Serve with the sour cream sauce and lemon wedges. *Makes 4 small moulds or 1 large mould.*

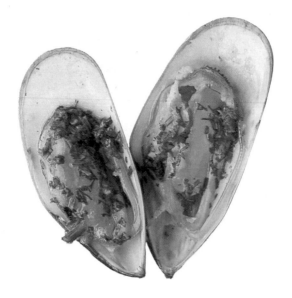

— HERB & GARLIC MUSSELS —

1 kg (2 lb) unshelled mussels
500 ml (16 fl oz/2 cups) water
125 g (4 oz) butter
2 cloves garlic, crushed
2 tablespoons chopped fresh parsley
1 tablespoon snipped fresh chives
1 tablespoon chopped fresh dill

Scrub the mussels well, removing the beards. Cover with cold water and soak for several hours. Discard any mussels with broken shells. Drain.

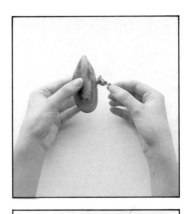

Bring the water to the boil in a frying pan. Add a layer of mussels and remove them once they open. Add more mussels as the cooked ones are removed. Discard any that do not open. Lift off the top shell of each mussel and discard. Beat the butter with the remaining ingredients.

Spread the herb butter over each of the mussels. Chill until ready to cook. Place under a hot grill until tops colour. Serve hot. *Makes about 30, depending on the size of the mussels.*

CUCUMBERS WITH MUSSELS

100 g (3½ oz) can smoked mussels or oysters
1 teaspoon lemon juice
few drops of Tabasco sauce
125 g (4 oz) high fat soft (cream) cheese
3 tablespoons finely chopped celery
1 cucumber (use long ones with few seeds)
salmon roe and fresh dill sprigs, to garnish

Drain oil from the mussels or oysters and place them in a bowl.

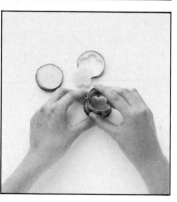

Add the lemon juice, Tabasco and cheese. Transfer to a food processor and blend well together. Turn into a bowl and stir in the chopped celery. Cover and chill the mixture until needed. Cut the cucumber into 1 cm (½ inch) thick slices. Stamp out with a fluted cutter and scoop a little flesh from the centre of each.

Spoon some of the mussel mixture on to each cucumber slice. Garnish with salmon roe and a dill sprig. Serve immediately. *Makes about 30.*

— OYSTERS WITH CAVIAR —

36 oysters on the shell
2 tablespoons thick mayonnaise or sour cream
salt and pepper
squeeze of lemon juice
1 teaspoon tomato paste
2 teaspoons bottled horseradish or to taste
3-4 tablespoons black caviar
fresh dill sprigs, to garnish

Arrange oysters on serving dishes and sit the dishes on ice.

Use a good mayonnaise. Season it with salt and pepper and stir in a squeeze of lemon juice and the tomato paste. Add the horseradish – the sauce should have a definite taste of horseradish so add more if needed.

Spoon a little of this sauce on each oyster. Top with the caviar and garnish with a dill sprig. Alternatively, the sauce may be served in a separate bowl with the caviar alongside for spooning over the oysters. *Makes 36.*

— OYSTERS ROCKEFELLER —

36 oysters on the shell
250 g (8 oz) packet frozen chopped spinach,
**   defrosted**
300 ml (10 fl oz) carton thick sour cream
2 cloves garlic, crushed
salt and pepper
3 tablespoons finely grated Cheddar cheese
30 g (1 oz/½ cup) soft breadcrumbs

Remove oysters from their shells. Drain the spinach well and place in a sieve. Press out as much moisture as possible.

Mix the sour cream with the garlic and stir in the spinach. Season well with salt and pepper. Put a teaspoon of this mixture in each oyster shell.

Return oysters to shells. Spoon the remaining spinach mixture over each. Mix the cheese and the breadcrumbs and sprinkle evenly over the oysters. Place under a hot grill until cheese melts and the crumbs turn golden. Serve hot. *Makes 36.*

— ANGELS ON HORSEBACK —

24 fresh or bottled oysters
½ lemon
1 tablespoon Worcestershire sauce
pepper
3 or 4 thin bacon rashers
lemon slices, to serve

Remove oysters from their shells, or drain if bottled. Squeeze the lemon juice over, add the Worcestershire sauce and a good grinding of black pepper. Marinate in the refrigerator for at least 1 hour.

Remove rind from the bacon rashers. Trim to 1 cm (½ in) widths and cut each rasher into pieces long enough to wrap around each oyster. The bacon trimmings can be used for other dishes.

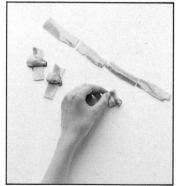

Place 1 oyster on each strip of bacon, roll the bacon around the oyster and secure with a toothpick. Refrigerate until ready to serve. Place bacon rolls in an ovenproof dish under a preheated grill or in an oven at 200C (400F/Gas 6) for 10 minutes or until bacon is crisp. Cool slightly and serve with slices of lemon. *Makes 24.*

SPANISH PRAWNS

500 g (1 lb) raw Mediterranean (king) prawns
6 tablespoons good olive oil or a mixture of olive
**   and vegetable oil**
1-2 small chillies, finely shredded
3 cloves garlic, crushed
salt
lemon wedges, to serve

Peel the prawns, leaving the tail intact. Cut along the back of each prawn, halfway through so it curls. Remove the vein.

Put the oil in a frying pan and add the chillies. Heat the oil until very hot, then add the prawns, garlic and salt, stirring until prawns are bright pink. Serve immediately with crusty bread and wedges of lemon. A bowl of Tartare Sauce may be placed alongside the prawns. *Serves 4.*

TARTARE SAUCE

6 tablespoons mayonnaise (use a good home-
**   made mayonnaise)**
3 spring onions, chopped
1 tablespoon drained capers
1 tablespoon finely chopped gherkins
1 tablespoon chopped fresh parsley

Combine all ingredients. Cover and chill until ready to serve with seafood.

GRILLED PRAWNS

8 raw Mediterranean (king) prawns, peeled
1 teaspoon olive or vegetable oil
2 tablespoons soy sauce
2 tablespoons ginger wine or dry sherry
squeeze of lemon juice
lemon slices, to serve

Remove the heads from the prawns. Cut each prawn along the back, taking care not to cut all the way through. Remove the vein.

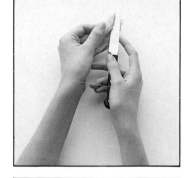

Open the prawns out flat and push a skewer through to hold each prawn open. Mix the oil, soy sauce, ginger wine and lemon juice together in a small bowl.

Brush the prawns with the soy sauce mixture. Grill on a barbecue or under a hot grill, basting constantly with the soy mixture until the prawns are cooked and well glazed. Alternatively, fry the prawns in an oiled frying pan, brushing with the soy mixture. Serve whole or cut into pieces with lemon slices. *Makes 8.*

SUSHI WITH PRAWNS

500 g (1 lb) short-grain rice
600 ml (20 fl oz/2½ cups) water
2 tablespoons mirin (sweet sake)
4 tablespoons rice vinegar
2 tablespoons sugar
2 teaspoons salt
24 cooked Mediterranean (king) prawns
2 teaspoons wasabi powder
nori (dried laver seaweed), if desired

Wash the rice several times in cold water and allow to drain well for 30 minutes. Put into a saucepan with the cold water. Bring to the boil, cover and steam over very low heat for 15 minutes. Heat mirin, vinegar, sugar and salt until boiling. Cool.

Remove rice from the heat and leave for 10 minutes. Turn rice into a large shallow dish and pour the vinegar dressing over. Mix gently but thoroughly until the rice reaches room temperature.

Shape the sushi into neat ovals and place on a serving platter. Peel the prawns, removing heads and leaving on the tails. Split down the underside – not all the way through – and flatten out. Wasabi is a very hot horseradish powder available from Asian food stores. Mix the powder with a few drops of water. Dab a little on the rice ovals and top each with a prawn. Wrap a strip of seaweed around each sushi if desired. *Makes 24.*

CELERY BOATS WITH PRAWNS

300 ml (10 fl oz) carton thick sour cream
1 tablespoon drained capers
1 tablespoon snipped fresh chives
2 tablespoons mild French mustard
500 g (1 lb) medium cooked prawns
3 or 4 sticks celery

Drain any liquid from the sour cream. If the cream is thin, whisk until it thickens. Chop the capers and add to the cream with the chives and mustard. Mix well. Chill.

Peel and de-vein the prawns. If large, cut each into 2 or 3 pieces.

Trim the celery and cut into 5 cm (2 in) lengths. Trim the rib of each length of celery so it will sit flat. Make sure the celery is well chilled and crisp. Spoon the sour cream mixture into each celery length and top with the prawns. Serve immediately. *Makes about 18.*

—— PRAWN VOL-AU-VENTS ——

30 g (1 oz) butter
2 tablespoons plain flour
315 ml (10 fl oz/1¼ cups) milk
60 g (2 oz) peeled prawns, chopped
squeeze of lemon juice
2 teaspoons snipped fresh chives
pinch of cayenne pepper
1 teaspoon paprika
salt
36 cocktail vol-au-vent (oyster) cases

Melt the butter in a saucepan, add the flour and stir well over a low heat for 2 minutes. Remove from heat and add the milk all at once.

Return to the heat and stir until the sauce boils and thickens. Remove from the heat. Add the prawns, lemon juice, chives, cayenne and paprika. Season to taste with salt. Cool the mixture slightly.

Spoon the prawn mixture into the vol-au-vent cases, then arrange on baking trays. Bake at 200C (400F/Gas 6) for 10 minutes. Cool slightly before serving. *Makes 36.*

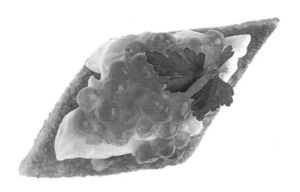

CROÛTONS WITH ROE
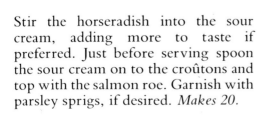

10 slices white bread
2 tablespoons vegetable oil
30 g (1 oz) butter
1-2 teaspoons bottled hot horseradish
125 ml (4 fl oz/½ cup) thick sour cream
3 tablespoons red salmon roe
fresh parsley sprig, optional

To make the croûtons, cut shapes out of sliced bread. Use shaped cutters for hearts and cut diamonds with a knife. Trimmings can be used for making breadcrumbs.

Heat oil and butter in a small frying pan. When hot, fry the bread pieces until they are golden, turning to colour both sides. Drain on absorbent paper and cool. The croûtons may be prepared ahead of time and stored in an airtight container.

Stir the horseradish into the sour cream, adding more to taste if preferred. Just before serving spoon the sour cream on to the croûtons and top with the salmon roe. Garnish with parsley sprigs, if desired. *Makes 20.*

TARAMASALATA

2 thick slices of crusty bread, weighing about
  180 g (6 oz)
125 g (4 oz) tarama (salted grey mullet roe)
1 clove garlic, crushed
1 tablespoon grated onion
1 egg yolk
2–3 tablespoons lemon juice
125 ml (4 fl oz/½ cup) olive oil
black olive and fresh chives, to garnish
crusty bread, to serve

Remove the crusts from the bread. Cover in cold water and soak for 10 minutes. Squeeze out the water.

Crumb the bread in a food processor. Remove. Place the tarama in the processor, add the garlic and onion and process until thoroughly mixed. Gradually add the breadcrumbs until the mixture is smooth. Blend in the egg yolk and 1 tablespoon of the lemon juice.

With the processor on, gradually pour in the olive oil, mixing until very creamy. Add more lemon juice to taste. Cover and chill. Garnish with a black olive and chives. Serve with crusty bread for dipping. *Serves 4 to 6.*
Note: Tarama is the salted roe from grey mullet and is available from many delicatessens, and larger super-markets.

SALMON MOUSSE

1 cucumber (use long one with few seeds)
440 g (14 oz) can red salmon, drained
1 tablespoon gelatine
125 ml (4 fl oz/½ cup) boiling water
½ teaspoon dry mustard
2 tablespoons white wine vinegar
1 teaspoon paprika
250 ml (8 fl oz/1 cup) single cream
lime slices, to serve

Trim the cucumber ends and cut lengthwise into thin slices using a mandolin or cutter. Line a long narrow 500 ml (16 fl oz/2 cup) loaf tin with the slices.

Mash salmon with a fork and remove any bones. Put the salmon flesh into a food processor and mix well. Dissolve the gelatine in the boiling water and pour over the salmon. Add the mustard, vinegar and paprika and blend well together until smooth.

Add the cream and blend until just mixed. Pour into the lined tin and chill until set. Turn out of the mould, cut into slices and serve on thin crisp-breads or biscuits with lime slices. *Serves 4 to 6.*

SALMON & AVOCADO MOUSSE

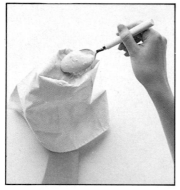

1 quantity Salmon Mousse, page 27, omitting cucumber
1 quantity Avocado Mousse, page 115
lettuce leaves and lime or lemon slices, to serve

Prepare the Salmon Mousse and pour into a 750 ml (24 fl oz/3 cup) tin lined with cling film (plastic wrap). The mousse should come half way up the side of the tin. Chill until beginning to set around the edges. Prepare the Avocado Mousse and put into a large piping bag with a plain tube.

Hold the nozzle of the piping bag below the surface of the Salmon Mousse and pipe in the avocado mixture, at the same time running the pipe along to the end of the loaf tin.

Chill the mousse until set. The mousse is easily removed from the tin by lifting the cling film. Serve slices on lettuce leaves. A spoonful of horseradish cream goes well with the mousse. *Serves 4 to 6.*

OPEN SALMON SANDWICHES

6 thin slices black, rye or sweet and sour bread
60 g (2 oz) butter, at room temperature
1 crisp, curly endive or lettuce, torn into small
    pieces
250 g (8 oz) thinly sliced smoked salmon
fresh dill sprigs and lemon twists, to garnish

Cut the bread into rounds using a biscuit cutter.

Spread the rounds liberally with butter. Top each round with the curly endive or lettuce.

Fold the salmon and arrange on top. Garnish with a dill sprig and a lemon twist. A dab of sour cream flavoured with chopped dill and chopped capers can be put on top, if desired. Serve immediately or chill briefly until ready to serve. *Makes 6.*

– SMOKED SALMON QUICHES –

½ x 375 g (12 oz) packet frozen puff pastry, defrosted
6 eggs
375 ml (12 fl oz/1½ cups) heavy (thickened) cream
½ teaspoon salt
pinch of grated nutmeg
125 g (4 oz) finely chopped smoked salmon
black caviar, extra salmon and dill sprigs, to garnish

Roll out the pastry thinly. Cut into 24 rounds with a 6.5 cm (2½ in) cutter. Line greased patty tins with the pastry rounds.

Beat the eggs with the cream, salt and nutmeg until well mixed. Stir in the salmon. Spoon the mixture into the pastry cases, ensuring the salmon is evenly distributed.

Bake at 200C (400F/Gas 6) for 10–15 minutes or until puffed and golden. Serve warm. For large parties, the quiches may be cooked in advance, removed from the tins and chilled. To re-heat, place on flat trays and warm at 200C (400F/Gas 6) for 5 minutes. *Makes 24.*

——— SALMON CANAPÉS ———

220 g (7 oz) can red salmon
½ teaspoon paprika
pepper
1 tablespoon cream
2 slices black bread
30 g (1 oz) butter
1 avocado
juice of 1 lemon
red caviar, to garnish

Drain the salmon, remove any bones and beat well with the paprika.

Flavour salmon with a good grinding of pepper. Gradually beat in the cream. Cut each slice of black bread into 4 triangles. Spread with butter. Pile the salmon mixture on to each piece of bread, smoothing with a knife.

Halve the avocado, remove stone and peel. Cut the flesh into slices, then again into smaller pieces. Place a piece of avocado on each salmon mound and squeeze the lemon juice over. Garnish with red caviar. *Makes 8.*

SALMON PUFFS

60 g (2 oz/½ cup) plain flour
125 ml (4 fl oz/½ cup) water
60 g (2 oz) butter, diced
½ teaspoon salt
30 g (1 oz) Cheddar cheese, finely grated
2 eggs
250 g (8 oz) can red salmon, drained
2 tablespoons mayonnaise
1 tablespoon sliced stuffed olives
red salmon roe or caviar, to garnish

Sift the flour on to a sheet of greaseproof paper. Heat the water and butter with salt until boiling.

Add the flour all at once to the water and stir over a low heat for about 1 minute, until the mixture leaves the sides of the pan and forms a ball. Remove from the heat, add the cheese and spread out on a plate to cool. Beat in the eggs, 1 at a time, until well blended.

When well combined, put small teaspoonfuls of the mixture on to a greased baking tray. Bake at 200C (400F/Gas 6) for 20 minutes, until puffed and golden. Cool. Combine the salmon with the mayonnaise and olives. Split the puffs and fill with the salmon mixture. Add a small amount of roe or caviar and serve immediately. *Serves 4 to 6.*

SQUID RINGS

500 g (1 lb) calamari or tender squid
2 or 3 lettuce leaves
2 sheets nori seaweed (optional)
125 ml (4 fl oz/½ cup) soy sauce
2 tablespoons water
2 tablespoons sugar
pickled ginger or lemon wedges, to serve

Pull the tentacles with ink bag and stomach attached away from the head of the squid. Cut the tentacles and remove the beak from the centre. Wash the tentacles and hood of the squid.

Put the lettuce leaves into a bowl and pour boiling water over. Drain well. Wrap all the tentacles tightly in the lettuce leaves, then enclose in the sheets of nori, sealing by lightly wetting the edge.

Stuff the tentacle bundle into the hood of the squid and seal the top with a skewer. In a saucepan, heat the soy sauce, water and sugar. Add the squid, and simmer for 20 to 30 minutes, turning occasionally, until tender. Cool, then chill. To serve, cut chilled squid into slices and accompany with pickled ginger or lemon wedges. *Makes about 20 slices.*

PICKLED SQUID

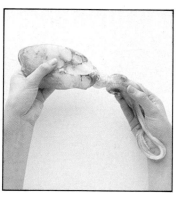

500 g (1 lb) squid
6 tablespoons olive or vegetable oil
3 tablespoons white wine
3 tablespoons white vinegar
2 cloves garlic
a few whole red chillies
salt and pepper

Pull the tentacles from the squid, carefully taking with them the stomach and ink bag.

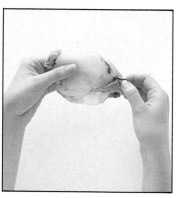

Wash the 'hood' or body and peel away the skin. Cut away the beak and ink bag from the tentacles and discard. Wash the tentacles well. Drop the tentacles and hood of the squid into a saucepan of boiling water. Return to the boil. As soon as the water boils, drain and rinse under cold water.

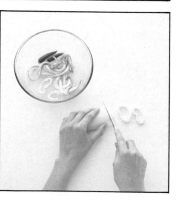

Slice the squid hood and put into a bowl with the tentacles and the remaining ingredients. Mix well. Cover and chill at least overnight, turning the squid occasionally so the flavours mingle. Lift the squid from the marinade and arrange in shallow serving dishes. *Makes about 20 slices.*

— CRISPY ALMOND SQUID —

500 g (1 lb) cleaned calamari bodies (hoods)
60 g (2 oz/½ cup) plain flour
salt and pepper
2 eggs, beaten
125 g (4 oz/1 cup) dry breadcrumbs
60 g (2 oz/½ cup) finely chopped unblanched
**   almonds**
vegetable oil for deep frying
lemon slices and fresh parsley sprigs, to serve

Slice the calamari into rings. If cleaned calamari are not available, buy the whole calamari and prepare according to the recipe for Pickled Squid, left.

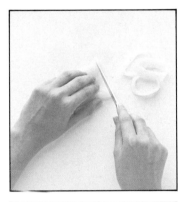

Season the flour with salt and pepper. Roll the calamari rings in the flour, then dip into the beaten egg. Mix the breadcrumbs with the almonds on a sheet of greaseproof paper. Roll the calamari rings in the breadcrumb mixture, making sure they are well coated. Chill on flat trays until ready to fry.

Heat oil for deep-frying and add a few calamari rings at a time. Fry until golden, remove with a slotted spoon and drain well. Overcooking will toughen the calamari. Continue to cook in small batches. Serve hot with lemon slices, and parsley sprigs. *Makes about 20 slices.*

— DEVILS ON HORSEBACK —

250 g (8 oz) prunes
125 g (4 oz) almonds
250 g (8 oz) bacon rashers, rinds removed
hot mango chutney, to serve

Originally the prunes would have been stuffed with hot chutney – hence the name 'devil' – but for ease we use almonds and serve the hot chutney alongside for dipping. Remove the stones from the prunes. Replace each stone with an almond.

Cut each bacon rasher into lengths just long enough to wrap around the prunes, and overlap slightly. Secure each with a wooden toothpick.

Cook under a hot grill until the bacon is crisp. Alternatively, arrange on baking tray and cook at 200C (400F/ Gas 6) for 10 to 15 minutes, until crisp. Serve with a bowl of hot mango chutney for dipping. *Makes about 30.*

BACON SANDWICHES

250 g (8 oz) bacon rashers
1 loaf sliced white or brown bread
1 bunch watercress
90 g (3 oz) butter
1 teaspoon prepared French mustard
pepper

Remove the rind from the bacon and grill the rashers until crisp. Drain and cool, then cut into small pieces.

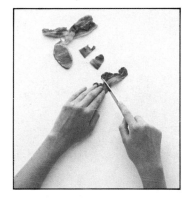

Cut each slice of bread with a round cutter. Use white or brown bread or a mixture of both. Wash the watercress and remove the tough stalks. Keep chilled until ready to use. Blend the butter with the French mustard until softened and spread one side of each round of bread with this mixture.

Place the watercress and bacon on half the bread rounds, grind some pepper over and top with the remaining bread rounds. If making the sandwiches a few hours in advance, cover with cling film (plastic wrap) and chill until ready to serve. Garnish the platter with sprigs of watercress. *Makes 12.*

BACON ROLLS

WATER CHESTNUTS WITH BACON

250 g (8 oz) can whole water chestnuts, drained
1 tablespoon soy sauce
1 teaspoon sugar
1 tablespoon white wine
4 bacon rashers, rinds removed

Marinate the water chestnuts in a mixture of soy, sugar and wine for at least 30 minutes. Wrap the chestnuts in strips of bacon. Grill until crisp.
Makes 12 to 15.

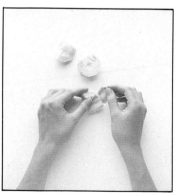

ARTICHOKES WITH BACON

400 g (14 oz) can artichoke hearts, drained and rinsed
4 or 5 bacon rashers, rinds removed

Cut each artichoke heart into halves or quarters. Wrap in strips of bacon. Grill until crisp. *Makes 12 to 16.*

MUSHROOMS WITH BACON

1 quantity Marinated Mushrooms, page 113, drained
10-12 bacon rashers, rinds removed

Wrap each mushroom in a bacon rasher which has been cut into pieces long enough to wrap around the mushrooms. Secure each with a toothpick. Grill until crisp. *Makes about 24.*

HAM CRESCENTS

125 g (4 oz) full fat soft (cream) cheese
125 g (4 oz) butter
125 g (4 oz/1 cup) plain flour
250 g (8 oz) cooked ham, finely minced
1 teaspoon prepared hot English mustard
2 tablespoons thick sour cream
1 egg, beaten, to glaze

Cream together the cheese and butter in a bowl until light. Work in the flour to form a dough. Knead lightly on a lightly floured surface. Wrap and chill.

Mix the ham, mustard and sour cream together in a bowl. Chill until ready to use. Roll out the pastry on a well-floured surface. (In hot weather, it is easier to roll between 2 sheets of cling film/plastic wrap). Cut into rounds using a 7.5 cm (3 in) cutter.

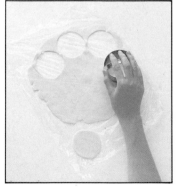

Put a heaped teaspoon of ham mixture on each pastry round. Brush the pastry edge with egg and fold over, then press to seal. Fork the joined edges and glaze with the egg. Pierce each pastry with the point of a knife to allow steam to escape. Place on a baking tray and bake at 200C (400F/ Gas 6) for 10 to 15 minutes, until golden. Serve hot. *Makes 20 to 24.*

HAM AND CHEESE CANAPÉS

10 bread slices
60 g (2 oz) butter
1 clove garlic, crushed
10 cooked ham slices
10 Gruyère cheese slices
**cherry tomatoes and fresh basil sprigs, to
garnish**

Toast the bread until golden on both
sides. While still hot, cut into rounds.

Cream the butter with the garlic.
Spread butter on one side of the toast
rounds. Cut the ham and the cheese
slices with the same cutter used to cut
the toast. Place the ham rounds on the
buttered toast. The trimmings can be
used in pies or for sandwich fillings.

Top the ham with the cheese rounds
and cook at 180C (350F/Gas 4) for 10
to 15 minutes or until the cheese melts.
Top with a cherry tomato and garnish
with a sprig of fresh basil. Serve hot.
Makes 10.

RIBBON SANDWICHES

1 loaf unsliced white bread, or use a mixture of
  brown and white bread
125 g (4 oz) butter
250 g (8 oz) cooked ham, chopped
3 tablespoons thick sour cream
2–3 teaspoons prepared mild mustard
2 teaspoons tomato paste
250 g (8 oz) cooked chicken meat
salt and pepper
2 tablespoons mayonnaise
2 tablespoons snipped fresh chives
1 teaspoon dried tarragon

Cut the bread into thin slices using an electric or serrated knife. Trim crusts and spread one side of each bread slice with butter.

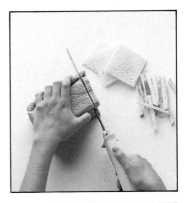

Mince the ham in a food processor. Stir in the sour cream, mustard and tomato paste. Mince the chicken and season with salt and pepper to taste. Stir in the mayonnaise, chives and the tarragon. Spread 10 slices of buttered bread with the chicken mixture, top each with another slice of bread.

Spread each top slice with the ham. Finish with the remaining bread slices, buttered side down. Wrap in cling film (plastic wrap). Refrigerate until ready to serve. Cut each sandwich into three fingers. *Makes 30.*

- HOT CHEESE & HAM PUFFS -

60 g (2 oz/½ cup) plain flour
125 ml (4 fl oz/½ cup)water
90 g (3 oz) butter, diced
½ teaspoon salt
2 eggs
1 tablespoon extra plain flour
125 ml (4 fl oz/½ cup) milk
3 tablespoons finely grated Cheddar cheese
60 g (2 oz) lean cooked ham, finely chopped
3 tablespoons grated fresh Parmesan cheese

Sift flour on to a sheet of greaseproof paper. Heat water and 60 g (2 oz) of the butter with salt until butter melts.

Bring mixture to a full boil and add flour all at once. Stir until mixture forms a ball and leaves the side of the pan. Cool. Beat in the eggs, one at a time. Drop heaped teaspoonfuls of mixture on to greased baking trays. Bake at 200C (400F/Gas 6) for 25 to 30 minutes, until puffed and golden. Cool, cut into halves and scoop out any soft centres.

Melt remaining butter in a small saucepan, stir in 1 tablespoon flour and cook for 1 minute. Add the milk and stir until sauce boils and thickens. Add the Cheddar cheese, then the ham. Season with salt and pepper. Spoon mixture into the puffs, replace tops and sprinkle with the Parmesan cheese. Return to the oven for 5 minutes to warm. *Makes about 20.*

SPRING ROLLS

250 g (8 oz) pork fillet
vegetable oil for deep–frying
1 small red pepper (capsicum), shredded
4 spring onions, chopped
100 g (3½ oz) fresh beansprouts
6 lettuce leaves, shredded
2 teaspoons cornflour
1 tablespoon soy sauce
½ teaspoon sugar
1 packet frozen spring roll pastry, defrosted and covered

Slice the pork thinly and cut crosswise into narrow shreds.

Heat 2 tablespoons oil in a frying pan. Fry the pork until it changes colour, then move it to one side of the pan. Add the pepper and spring onions and cook, stirring, for 3 minutes. Add the bean sprouts and lettuce. Blend the cornflour with 1 tablespoon cold water. Stir into the mixture in the pan, heating until it boils and thickens. Stir in the soy sauce and sugar. Cool.

Peel off one spring roll wrapper at a time and put 2 tablespoons of the filling in the centre of each. Fold one corner over the filling, then tuck in the sides and roll up, sealing with water. Repeat with remaining pastries. Deep–fry rolls a few at a time in hot oil until golden. Drain. Serve hot with chilli sauce. *Makes 20.*

— CHINESE DUMPLINGS —

125 g (4 oz) won ton wrappers
250 g (8 oz) can bamboo shoots
4 spring onions
250 g (8 oz) lean minced pork
½ teaspoon grated fresh root ginger
1 teaspoon salt
1 egg white
2 teaspoons soy sauce
plum or chilli sauce for dipping

Won ton wrappers can be purchased from Asian food shops. Finely chop the bamboo shoots and the spring onions.

Combine these vegetables with the pork, ginger, salt, egg white and soy sauce. Mix together well. Put one heaped teaspoonful of this mixture on each won ton square, keeping the unused squares covered with a damp piece of absorbent paper.

Squeeze the pastry around the filling to resemble a money bag. Place without the dumplings touching each other, in an oiled bamboo steaming basket. Steam over boiling water for 20 minutes. Serve hot with plum sauce or chilli for dipping. *Makes about 20.*

— SPICY PORK ROLLS —

250 g (8 oz) pork fillet
6 or 7 spring onions
1 clove garlic, crushed
1 tablespoon dark soy sauce
1 tablespoon honey
1 tablespoon oil
1 tablespoon hoi sin sauce
1 teaspoon grated fresh root ginger

Trim any fat and sinew from the pork and cut the fillets crosswise into 20 thin slices.

Gently pound the meat with a knife to flatten. Trim the spring onions and cut into short lengths. Combine the remaining ingredients in a shallow ovenproof dish and mix well.

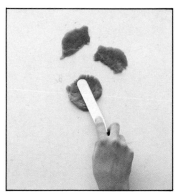

Roll each slice of meat around a piece of spring onion. The moisture in the meat will keep the rolls intact. Place the pork rolls in the soy mixture. If preparing ahead of serving time, cover and chill. Cook at 200C (400F/Gas 6) for 10 to 15 minutes, basting with the sauce as they cook. Serve hot or warm. *Makes 20.*

— SALAMI CRESCENTS —

**2 sheets frozen puff pastry or 375 g (12 oz) frozen
   block puff pastry
2 tablespoons sour cream
1 teaspoon hot prepared mustard
8 slices mettwurst salami
8 slices Emmenthal (Swiss) cheese
1 egg, beaten, to glaze**

Cut each sheet of pastry into quarters
so each square measures 17.5 cm (7 in).
If using a block of puff pastry, roll out
thinly and cut into eight 17.5 cm (7 in)
squares.

Mix the sour cream and mustard and
spread evenly over the pastry squares,
taking the mixture almost to the edges
of the pastry. Cut the salami and cheese
slices into halves. Place on the pastry
and cut each square of pastry
diagonally into halves, then into
quarters.

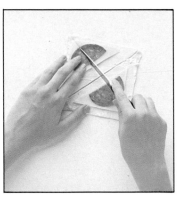

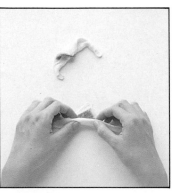

Starting from the wide side of each
triangle, roll up the filling in the
pastry. Place on greased baking sheets
and bend the pastries gently into
crescent shapes. Brush with the beaten
egg. Bake at 200C (400F/Gas 6) for 10
to 15 minutes or until golden. Serve
hot. *Makes 32.*

— LIVERWURST CANAPÉS —

2 small loaves crusty French bread
3 tablespoons olive oil
2 tablespoons melted butter
1 small clove garlic, crushed
250 g (8 oz) smoked liverwurst
6 thin slices Emmenthal (Swiss) cheese, cut into
  squares
6–12 pickled dill cucumbers

Choose the narrow French loaves that will cut into smaller rounds. Slice bread into 1 cm (½ in) thick rounds.

Mix the oil and butter with the garlic. Brush bread slices on both sides with butter mixture. Place in one layer in a shallow ovenproof dish and cook at 200C (400F/Gas 6) for 10 minutes, until golden and crispy on the edges.

Mix the liverwurst until it softens and spread evenly on each slice of bread. Top each with a piece of cheese. Return to the oven for 5 to 10 minutes, until the cheese melts. Serve hot with a piece of dill pickle on each. *Makes about 24.*

SATAY SAUSAGE ROLLS

1 onion, finely chopped
1 tablespoon vegetable oil
1 tablespoon dark soy sauce
2 teaspoons lemon juice
2 cloves garlic, crushed
1 teaspoon hot chilli sauce
750 g (1½ lb) sausage-meat
3 eggs
2 x 375 g (12 oz) packets frozen puff pastry

Gently cook the onion in the oil over a low heat. Add soy sauce, lemon juice, garlic and chilli sauce.

Add the sausage-meat and 2 of the eggs to the onion mixture. Mix all well together. Roll out half the pastry on a lightly floured surface to 20 x 25 cm (8 x 10 in) rectangle. Cut lengthwise into 2 strips. Repeat with the other packet of pastry.

Pile sausage filling down the centre of each pastry strip. Beat the remaining egg. Brush edges of the pastry with the beaten egg. Fold pastry over and join to form a roll. Slash the top of the pastry and cut each roll into 4 cm (1½ in) lengths. Put rolls on baking sheets and bake at 200C (400F/Gas 6) until golden, about 20 minutes. Serve hot with a spicy sauce. *Makes 40.*

—— LIVERWURST BALLS ——

2 rashers bacon, rind removed
1 small onion, finely chopped
250 g (8 oz) liverwurst
2 tablespoons brandy or Grand Marnier
1 large bunch of fresh parsley, finely chopped
shredded orange rind and nuts, to garnish

Finely dice the bacon. Fry bacon over a low heat, stirring until beginning to crisp. Remove the bacon. Add the onion to the pan and fry in the bacon fat over a low heat until transparent.

Put bacon, onion and liverwurst into a bowl. Warm the brandy or Grand Marnier, ignite and pour over the liverwurst. Mix together well. Chill to firm.

Put the chopped parsley on a sheet of greaseproof paper. Take heaped teaspoonfuls of the liverwurst mixture and roll into balls. Roll the balls in the parsley. Chill balls until ready to serve. If using brandy, a nut may garnish each ball. If using Grand Marnier, garnish with finely shredded orange rind. *Makes 12 to 15 balls.*

—— BARBECUED CSABAI ——

4 csabai sausages (not the csabai salami which is much harder)

This appetiser makes an ideal start to a barbecue because not only is the taste delicious, but the flavour from the sausages penetrates the meats which are cooked later. The sausage can be grilled or fried on the oven. Cut the csabai into finger lengths and peel.

Split each piece of csabai lengthwise into halves. Cover and refrigerate until ready to cook.

Prepare the barbecue in advance so the coals are glowing. Grease the grid lightly with oil and place the csabai, cut side down, on the barbecue. Alternatively, use a frying pan over a moderate heat. Cook until coloured, turn and cook the other side. Cut into chunks and serve hot. *Makes about 50 pieces.*

— PIROSHKI WITH THYME —

60 g (2 oz) fresh (compressed) yeast
2 tablespoons sugar
315 ml (10 fl oz/1¼ cups) lukewarm milk
375 g (12 oz/3 cups) plain flour
salt and pepper
180 g (6 oz) butter, melted
3 large onions, chopped
250 g (8 oz) bacon
1 egg, beaten, to glaze
2 tablespoons fresh thyme leaves

Cream yeast with the sugar. Stir in the milk.

In a large bowl, mix flour and 2 teaspoons salt and make a well in the centre. Pour the yeast mixture and 125 g (4 oz) melted butter into the centre. Beat well for 3 minutes to form a smooth batter. Cover with cling film (plastic wrap) and leave in a warm place for 1 hour or until double in bulk. Gently sauté onions in remaining butter until golden. Cool. Chop bacon finely and add to the onions with 1 teaspoon pepper and the thyme.

Knead dough lightly, then divide into 35 to 40 portions. Wrap a teaspoon of the bacon filling in each portion of dough. Prove in a warm place on greased trays for 15 minutes. Brush with egg. Bake at 230C (450F/Gas 8) for 10 to 15 minutes. *Makes 35 to 40.*

— PARMA HAM ROULADES —

60 g (2 oz) Ricotta cheese
60 g (2 oz) Stilton cheese
1 tablespoon thick sour cream
12 very thin slices Parma ham (prosciutto) or coppa or ham deluxe
1 pear, apple or fresh fig

Blend both cheeses with the sour cream. Spread evenly on the thin slices of Parma ham (prosciutto), taking the mixture almost to the edges.

Peel the pear, cut into quarters and remove the core, then thinly slice. Place a piece of pear on each cheese-topped slice of prosciutto.

Roll up the ham. Place on a dish, cover and chill until ready to serve. Apples or fresh figs, when in season, may be used instead of the pear. Peel and slice the figs before using. *Makes 12*.

RUMAKI

500 g (1 lb) chicken livers
2 tablespoons vegetable oil
1 tablespoon soy sauce
1 tablespoon dry sherry
squeeze of lemon juice
1 clove garlic, crushed
10 canned water chestnuts, drained and sliced
about 12 bacon rashers

Halve the livers, removing connective tissue and any dark spots. Heat the oil in a frying pan and gently cook the livers, 1 layer at a time, turning constantly, until they change colour.

Remove from the heat. Add soy, sherry, lemon juice and garlic. Mix well. Cool. Remove bacon rinds. Cut each rasher into 2 or 3 pieces.

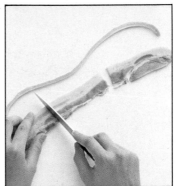

Place a piece of chicken liver on a strip of bacon and top with a slice of water chestnut. Roll up and secure with a toothpick. Repeat until all chicken livers are used. Chill until ready to serve. To serve, grill until bacon is crisp or bake at 200C (400F/Gas 6) for about 10 minutes. Serve hot. *Makes about 28.*

- CHICKEN & SAUSAGE ROLLS -

500 g (1 lb) skinned chicken breasts (fillets)
salt and pepper
2 or 3 peperoni sausages
12 green beans, topped and tailed
6 sheets filo pastry
125 g (4 oz) butter, melted
mango chutney, if desired

Split the chicken breasts. Place a sheet of cling film (plastic wrap) over the breasts and beat them out thinly. Season with salt and pepper.

Peel skin from the sausages and cut into lengths the same size as the chicken. Place two beans alongside a strip of sausage on each chicken piece. Roll the chicken around the sausage. Brush 1 sheet of pastry with melted butter and fold into quarters.

Place 1 chicken roll in the centre of the folded pastry and roll up, tucking in the sides. Place in a shallow baking tray. Brush with more butter. Make remaining pastries in the same way. Bake at 200C (400F/Gas 6) for 15 to 20 minutes, until golden. Cut into chunks. Serve hot, accompanied with a bowl of mango chutney. *Makes about 30.*

CHICKEN SATAY

500 g (1 lb) skinned chicken breasts (fillets)
½ teaspoon sambal olek
1 teaspoon grated fresh root ginger
2 tablespoons lemon juice
3 tablespoons dark soy sauce
2 tablespoons honey
1 tablespoon peanut butter
125 ml (4 fl oz/½ cup) water
cherries and fresh parsley sprigs, to garnish

Cut the chicken into 2.5 cm (1 in) cubes and thread on to 15 bamboo skewers.

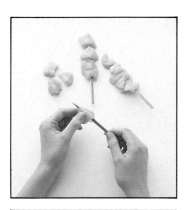

Put remaining ingredients, except the cherries and parsley, into a large frying pan or saucepan and heat, stirring well. Bring to the boil, then lower heat and add chicken skewers, cooking 1 layer at a time. Simmer for 10 minutes, basting occasionally, then remove chicken.

Repeat until all the skewers of chicken are cooked, basting from time to time. Simmer the sauce in the pan until it has reduced to about 180 ml (6 fl oz/¾ cup). Pour this over the chicken. Chill. The skewers may be garnished with cherries and fresh parsley sprigs. Serve cold. *Makes 15.*

SESAME CHICKEN

500 g (1 lb) skinned chicken breasts (fillets)
1 teaspoon salt
2 tablespoons light soy sauce
2 tablespoons maple syrup
2 tablespoons ginger wine
½ teaspoon five-spice powder
2 tablespoons oil
2 tablespoons sesame seeds
chutney or Chinese plum, to serve (optional)

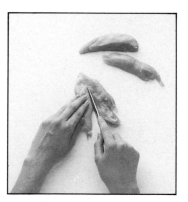

Cut each chicken breast lengthwise in half.

Combine salt, soy sauce, maple syrup, ginger wine, five-spice powder and oil in an ovenproof dish. Add the chicken and turn to coat evenly with the marinade. Cover and marinate for 2 hours, turning occasionally. The chicken may be refrigerated for several hours in the marinade until shortly before serving.

Sprinkle marinated chicken with sesame seeds. Bake at 200C (400F/Gas 6) for 15 minutes, brushing from time to time with the marinade. Cut the chicken into pieces. Serve warm or cold with a bowl of chutney or Chinese plum sauce if desired. *Makes about 24 pieces.*

YAKITORI

250 g (8 oz) skinned chicken breasts (fillets)
6 spring onions
2 tablespoons sake
2 tablespoons light soy sauce
½ teaspoon grated fresh root ginger
2 teaspoons sugar

Cut the chicken pieces into small cubes.

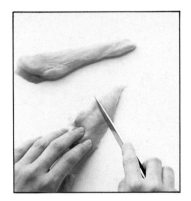

Wash and trim the spring onions and cut them into 4 cm (1½ in) lengths, using some of the green tops. Thread the chicken cubes and spring onions alternately on to 6 bamboo skewers.

Heat the sake and add the remaining ingredients. Place the skewers on the grill tray and cover the exposed ends of the skewers with a sheet of foil. Brush the sake mixture over chicken and onions. Grill until the chicken is cooked, brushing with the marinade and turning occasionally. Cook for about 6 minutes, until the chicken is cooked through. Serve hot. *Makes 6.*

— CHICKEN & LEEK ROLLS —

375 g (12 oz) skinned chicken breasts (fillets)
2 leeks
3 tablespoons dark soy sauce
1 tablespoon ginger wine
2 teaspoons sugar
2 tablespoons vegetable oil
125 ml (4 fl oz/½ cup) water

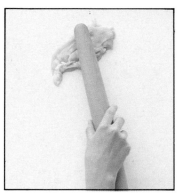

Beat out chicken with a rolling pin until each is a thin, even layer.

Cut leeks into quarters and wash well to remove grit. Place lengthwise down the centre of each chicken piece and roll up. Secure with a skewer. Marinate the rolls in a mixture of 2 tablespoons of the soy sauce, the ginger wine and sugar.

Heat oil and fry chicken rolls until they are brown on all sides. Add remaining soy sauce and the water to the pan. Cover and simmer for 10 minutes or until the chicken is cooked through and tender. Remove skewers and cut into chunks. Serve hot or cold. *Makes about 30.*

— LIVER-PISTACHIO PÂTÉ —

250 g (8 oz) chicken livers
125 g (4 oz) butter
1 small onion, chopped
1 clove garlic, chopped
2 tablespoons Cognac or brandy
2 tablespoons single cream
90 g (3 oz/½ cup) whole pistachio nuts
extra 2-3 tablespoons melted butter and extra
**   pistachio nuts, to garnish**
Melba toast, to serve

Carefully pick over the livers, discarding any dark spots or green particles. Simmer livers in 500 ml (16 fl oz/2 cups) water for 5 minutes. Drain. Melt half the butter and gently sauté the onion and garlic without browning. Add the drained livers. Sauté until they are cooked through, stirring constantly. Cool.

Blend the livers until smooth in a food processor. Melt the remaining butter. Add butter, Cognac and cream to the liver mixture. Stir in the nuts.

Pour mixture into 6 to 8 individual ramekins and chill. Pour a thin layer of melted butter over each, sprinkle with more nuts and chill again. Serve with Melba toast. *Makes 6 to 8 ramekins.*

— GLAZED CHICKEN WINGS —

750 g (1½ lb) chicken wings
3 spring onions
3 tablespoons ginger wine
4 tablespoons dark soy sauce
2 teaspoons sugar
sesame seeds

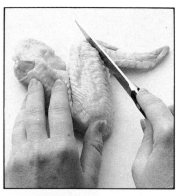

Remove the tips from the chicken wings. These can be used to make stock for soup. The wings may be left or cut again at the joint into half.

Cut the spring onion into 5 cm (2 in) lengths and put into a large saucepan or a wok with the ginger wine and soy sauce. Add the sugar and bring to the boil. Place the chicken wings, in 1 layer, in this mixture.

Cover and simmer slowly for 20 minutes or until chicken is cooked through and tender when tested with a skewer. Turn the chicken over from time to time. Serve warm or cold. If liked, sprinkle with sesame seeds. *Makes 8 to 10.*

—— SMOKED BEEF TARTS ——

125 g (4 oz/1 cup) plain flour
1 tablespoon grated fresh Parmesan cheese
60 g (2 oz) butter
1 egg, beaten
salt
440 g (14 oz) can artichoke hearts
125 g (4 oz) thinly sliced smoked beef
2 tablespoons sour cream
2 teaspoons chopped fresh dill sprigs
fresh dill sprigs and red pepper (capsicum)
   strips, to garnish

Sift flour, stir in cheese and rub in the butter. Make a well in the centre, add the egg and salt. Form into a dough and knead lightly. Chill.

Roll out the pastry thinly between sheets of cling film (plastic wrap) lightly dusted with flour. Cut into rounds with a cutter and line small greased tins. Chill. Prick well with a fork and bake at 200C (400F/Gas 6) for 10 to 15 minutes, until golden. Cool. Store in an airtight container until ready to serve.

Drain the artichoke hearts well and rinse in cold water. Cut into quarters or dice if the artichokes are large. Cut the beef into strips and roll each strip into a cylinder. Mix the sour cream with the dill. Spoon a little sour cream into each pastry case and top with the artichoke and smoked beef. Serve immediately. Garnish with dill sprigs and red pepper strips. *Makes about 15.*

— MINTED MEATBALLS —

1 kg (2 lb) lean minced beef
3 eggs
2 onions, finely chopped
90 g (3 oz/1½ cups) soft breadcrumbs
3 tablespoons lemon juice
2 tablespoons chopped fresh mint
2 cloves garlic, crushed
2 teaspoons salt
vegetable oil for frying

Combine meat with all other ingredients, except the oil. Using wet hands, form into 40 balls.

Pour 1 cm (½ in) deep oil in a pan, and heat. Fry the meatballs, 1 layer at a time, turning constantly. Drain. Serve hot, garnished with mint sprigs, with Minted Yogurt Sauce. The meatballs can be cooked successfully ahead of serving and chilled or frozen. Reheat in oven before serving. *Makes 40.*

MINTED YOGURT SAUCE

6 spring onions, finely chopped
200 g (7 oz) carton plain yogurt
3 tablespoons chopped fresh mint
2 teaspoons grated fresh root ginger
1 clove garlic, crushed
fresh mint sprig, to garnish

Combine spring onions and yogurt. Stir in remaining ingredients and store in the refrigerator. Serve alongside the meatballs for dipping.

— OPEN BEEF SANDWICHES —

4 egg yolks
250 g (8 oz) butter
2 teaspoons dried tarragon
1 tablespoon white vinegar
1 teaspoon green peppercorns, drained
1 loaf crusty French bread
lettuce leaves (optional)
about 500 g (1 lb) rare roast beef

Blend the yolks in a food processor or blender. Melt the butter with the tarragon and, while still very hot, gradually add to the egg yolks, blending all the time. Add the vinegar and mix well.

Turn off the processor and stir in the green peppercorns. Unlike the traditional Béarnaise sauce, this one needs to be chilled before serving - chilling improves the texture. It will keep refrigerated for 1 week. Cut bread in thick slices. Top each slice with a lettuce leaf, if used.

Cut the beef into 20 thin slices. Place on bread, allowing two small slices for each open sandwich, but one if the slices are large. Spoon a little of the Béarnaise Sauce on top and garnish as liked. Serve at once. *Makes 10.*

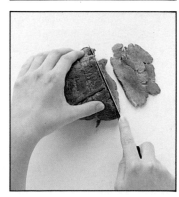

—CURRANT MEATBALLS—

500 g (1 lb) lean finely minced beef
30 g (1 oz/½ cup) soft white breadcrumbs
125 ml (4 fl oz/½ cup) cream
1 small onion, finely chopped
pinch of ground cloves
½ teaspoon ground cinnamon
1 egg
2 teaspoons salt
60 g (2 oz) currants
60 g (2 oz) toasted pine nuts
2 tablespoons vegetable oil
fresh basil sprigs, to garnish

Put the minced beef into a bowl. Soak the breadcrumbs in the cream for 5 minutes, then add to the meat.

Stir in the onion, spices, egg, salt, currants and pine nuts. Mix together well. Form into 20 small meatballs, rolling with wet hands.

Heat the oil in a frying pan and cook the meatballs, 1 layer at a time, until browned all over. Serve hot, garnished with basil sprigs. The meatballs may be fried ahead of time and kept in the refrigerator. To reheat, place in a shallow ovenproof dish and warm in an oven preheated to 180C (350F/Gas 4) for about 10 minutes. *Makes 20.*

— SMOKED BEEF CANAPÉS —

10 slices black or dark (heavy) rye bread
60 g (2 oz) butter
20–30 thin slices smoked beef
250 ml (8 fl oz/1 cup) thick, homemade
  mayonnaise
125 g (4 oz) canned tuna, drained
juice of ½ lemon
1 teaspoon drained capers
lemon twists, extra capers, onion slices and fresh
  dill sprigs, to garnish

Cut the bread into halves and spread
with the butter. Arrange the beef slices
on the buttered bread.

To make the tuna sauce, put the
mayonnaise, tuna, lemon juice and
capers into a blender or food
processor. Process until well blended.

Spoon the sauce on the smoked beef.
Garnish with extra capers, a few onion
slices, a dill sprig and a lemon twist. If
preparing in advance, the buttered
bread can be covered and refrigerated
and the canapés assembled just before
serving. *Makes 20.*

CURRY PIES

1 onion, chopped
1 tablespoon vegetable oil
1 tablespoon curry powder
2 tablespoons vinegar
6 tablespoons water
500 g (1 lb) lean minced beef
1 teaspoon salt
2 tablespoons sultanas
2 teaspoons cornflour
250 g (8 oz) shortcrust pastry
water or 1 egg, beaten, to glaze

Sauté the onion in the oil for 2 minutes, stirring, until soft.

Add the curry powder and stir for 1 more minute. Add the vinegar, 4 tablespoons water and mix well. Stir in the meat, salt and sultanas, then cook for 10 minutes. Blend the cornflour with the remaining 2 tablespoons water and stir into the mixture. Cook for a further 2 minutes. Cool, then chill.

Thinly roll pastry out and cut into rounds to fit 12 to 15 greased tins. Spoon the curry mixture in the pastry cases and top with another pastry round, pressing edges with a fork to seal. Brush with water or egg to glaze and bake at 200C (400F/Gas 6) for approximately 15 minutes, until golden. Cool slightly and serve. *Makes 12 to 15.*

- BLUE CHEESE MUSHROOMS -

12 to 14 button mushrooms
125 g (4 oz) blue cheese
125 g (4 oz) full fat soft (cream) cheese
1 tablespoon single cream
pecan nuts and fresh basil or parsley sprigs, to garnish

Wipe the mushroom with a clean cloth dipped in cold water to which a few slices of lemon or a few drops of white vinegar has been added.

Cut out the stalks from the mushrooms (They can be used for cooking). Soften the cheeses and beat together until smooth, then beat in the cream. Put into a piping bag fitted with a star nozzle. If preparing ahead, place the mushrooms, covered, and the bag with the filling, in the refrigerator until just before serving.

Pipe the cheese mixture into the mushrooms. Top each with a nut and a basil or parsley sprig. *Makes 12 to 14.*

CHEESE STRAWS

90 g (3 oz) butter
90 g (3 oz/¾ cup) grated Cheddar cheese
125 g (4 oz/1 cup) plain flour
1 teaspoon paprika
good pinch of cayenne pepper

Preheat the oven to 180C (350F/Gas 4).
Cream the butter until light, then beat
in the grated cheese.

Sift the flour and blend into the
creamed butter mixture to make a
dough. Divide dough into balls, wrap
each in cling film (plastic wrap) and
chill until firm enough to roll. Roll out
the dough between two sheets of cling
film, dusted with a little flour. This
makes the rolling of very short
mixtures, such as this, much easier,
particularly during hot weather.

Roll the dough to 3 mm (⅛ in) thick
and cut into 10 cm (4 in) lengths, each
1 cm (½ in) wide. Place the cheese
sticks on to baking trays and turn each
end twice to give each stick 2 twists.
Mix the paprika with the cayenne and,
using a dry brush, dab the paprika on
to the twists. Bake for 10 minutes.
Makes about 80.

— HERBED CHEESE BITES —

250 g (8 oz) Cheddar cheese
6–10 rashers bacon
40 fresh sage or basil leaves

Cut the cheese into 40 cubes. Trim the rind from the bacon and cut into lengths long enough to wrap around the cheese. Use bacon trimmings in other dishes.

Wrap a sage leaf around each piece of cheese. Enclose in a piece of bacon and secure with wooden toothpicks. Place in a greased frying pan and cook over a moderate heat until bacon is crisp. Cool slightly and serve hot or warm.

CHEESE AND PEPERONI BITES

Omit the sage leaves and replace with a slice of peperoni salami. Follow the method above and serve in the same way. *Makes 40.*

- CHEESE & ONION PASTRIES -

180 g (6 oz/1½ cups) plain flour
½ teaspoon salt
125 ml (4 fl oz/½ cup) cold water
24 spring onions
30 g (1 oz) butter
good pinch of cayenne pepper
125 g (4 oz) Gouda cheese, cut into 24 cubes
1 egg, beaten
vegetable oil for deep-frying

Sift the flour with the salt, then add the water to make a firm dough. Knead for 5 minutes, until smooth. Wrap and leave to rest for 30 minutes.

Chop the spring onions, including most of the green tops; there should be about 250 g (8 oz/1 cup). Gently sauté onions in the butter until softened. Remove from the heat and add the cayenne pepper. Shape the dough into 24 balls and roll each out into a circle about 10 cm (4 in) wide.

Spoon a little spring onion mixture on to each pastry circle, top with a cheese cube and brush edges with the beaten egg. Fold pastry over the filling. Press edges together with a fork to seal. Deep-fry the pastries, a few at a time, in hot oil until golden. Drain and serve warm. *Makes 24.*

— SESAME CHEESE BALLS —

60 g (2 oz) sesame seeds
60 g (2 oz) pepitas or slivered almonds
250 g (8 oz) full fat soft (cream) cheese
2 tablespoons grated Parmesan cheese
2 teaspoons dried onion flakes
salt and pepper

Stir the sesame seeds in a dry frying pan over a moderate heat until they turn golden. Remove to a plate to cool. Put the pepitas or almonds on a baking tray and roast at 180C (350F/ Gas 4) for 10 minutes. Cool.

Beat the cheeses and onion flakes well together. Season with salt and pepper to taste. Stir the sesame seeds into the cheese mixture and roll into 25 balls.

Place the toasted pepitas on a sheet of greaseproof paper and roll the cheese balls in the pepitas. Store in the refrigerator or a cool place until ready to serve. *Makes 25.*

— ALMOND CHEESE BALLS —

**250 g (8 oz/2 cups) grated mature Cheddar
   cheese**
4 tablespoons plain flour
2 egg whites
180 g (6 oz/1 cup) blanched almonds
vegetable oil for deep-frying

Combine the cheese and the flour. Beat
the egg whites until they form stiff
peaks.

Add the cheese and flour to the egg
whites and fold in gently. Form into 16
to 18 small balls, gently rolling
between your fingers.

Roll the cheese balls in the almonds.
The cheese balls may be refrigerated
until needed. Heat the oil and cook the
cheese balls, a few at a time, until
golden all over. Take care not to have
the oil too hot or the almonds will
brown before the centre is hot. Drain
on absorbent paper and serve. *Makes
16 to 18.*

— PEPPER CHEESE ROUNDS —

250 g (8 oz) mature Cheddar cheese
250 g (8 oz) full fat soft (cream) cheese, at room temperature
60 ml (2 fl oz/¼ cup) dry sherry
6 tablespoons coarsely cracked black peppercorns

Grate the Cheddar cheese into a bowl. Beat with the full fat soft cheese until well blended, then beat in the sherry.

Chill the mixture until firm and divide into four portions. Shape each into a log by rolling in a piece of cling film (plastic wrap). Alternatively, the cheese can be shaped into rounds.

Roll each log in the peppercorns, gently pressing the peppers into the cheese. Chill until ready to serve. Slice and serve plain or on a croûton, if desired, topped with a slice of tomato or a prawn. Accompany with biscuits (crackers), celery sticks and radishes. *Makes 4 logs.*

APRICOT CHEESE

250 g (8 oz) full fat soft (cream) cheese
90 g (3 oz) ready-to-eat dried apricots
60 g (2 oz) hazelnuts
4 tablespoons poppy seeds or toasted sesame seeds

Soften the cheese at room temperature and beat with a wooden spoon until smooth. Cut apricots into small chunks and add to the cheese.

Place the hazelnuts on a baking tray and place in an oven at 200C (400F/Gas 6) for 10 minutes. Remove from the oven and rub between several thicknesses of absorbent paper to remove skins. Return the nuts to the oven for a further 5 minutes or until golden. Chop roughly and mix with the cheese.

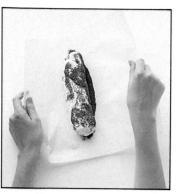

Form the cheese, on a sheet of greaseproof (wax) paper, in the shape of a 20 cm (8 in) long log. Roll the log in the poppy seeds to coat it thoroughly. Chill until firm. Serve sliced on a board with biscuits (crackers) or apple pieces. *Makes about 20 slices.*

—— BASIL-CHEESE TOASTS ——

2 tomatoes
45 g (1½ oz) canned flat anchovy fillets, well
  drained
10 slices French bread
125 g (4 oz) Gruyère cheese
pepper
4 tablespoons finely shredded basil leaves
4 tablespoons olive oil
10 calamatta olives, if desired
fresh basil leaves, to garnish

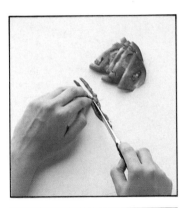

Slice the tomatoes thinly; if the tomatoes are large, halve the slices. Cut the anchovies into long strips.

Place the bread in a shallow oiled ovenproof dish. Grate the cheese and divide among the slices of French bread. Arrange the anchovy strips on top, then add a tomato slice or two. Grind some pepper over and sprinkle with some of the fresh basil.

Drizzle the olive oil over and cook at 200C (400F/Gas 6) for 10 to 15 minutes, until the bread is crisp and the cheese has melted. Sprinkle the remaining basil over and place a calamatta olive on top of each, if desired. Serve hot. *Makes 10.*

– SAGE & ONION PINWHEELS –

250 g (8 oz) full fat soft (cream) cheese
30 fresh sage leaves
3 tablespoons chopped spring onions
pepper

Soften the cheese and spread out on a sheet of foil to a 20 cm (8 in) square.

Lay the fresh sage leaves evenly over the cheese. If the sage is too dry and strong tasting, substitute chopped parsley, basil leaves or any other suitable fresh herb. Sprinkle with the spring onions and generously grind black pepper over the top.

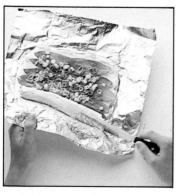

Using the foil as a guide, roll up the cheese, making a tight log. Chill until firm or ready to serve. Cut into slices. Serve plain or on biscuits (crackers) or Melba toast. *Makes 18 to 20.*

— CHEESE-FILO PASTRIES —

500 g (1 lb) feta cheese
3 tablespoons chopped fresh parsley
pepper
3 eggs, beaten
8 sheets filo pastry
125 g (4 oz) butter, melted

Crumble the cheese into a bowl. Mix together the parsley, pepper and beaten eggs. Stir into the cheese and mix together well.

Take 1 sheet of pastry and cut in half, keeping the remainder of the pastry covered with damp absorbent paper to prevent it drying out. Brush the pastry with melted butter and fold into quarters. Put a spoonful of the filling in the centre of each.

Squeeze the pastry around the filling to resemble a money bag (they may be cooked in buttered patty cake tins). Brush pastry with any remaining butter. Bake at 200C (400F/Gas 6) for 20 to 25 minutes, until golden. Serve hot. *Makes 16.*

POTTED CHEESE

250 g (8 oz) Cheddar cheese
60 g (2 oz) blue cheese
30 g (1 oz) butter
2 tablespoons dry sherry
½ teaspoon Worcestershire sauce
¼ teaspoon hot English mustard
1 tablespoon finely chopped fresh herbs
Melba toast or biscuits (crackers), to serve

Grate the Cheddar cheese into a bowl.
Add the blue cheese, mixing together
with a fork.

Soften the butter and add to the cheese.
Blend together well. Gradually beat
in the sherry, Worcestershire sauce,
mustard and herbs. Blend in a food
processor until smooth and thoroughly mixed.

Pack into a serving bowl, cover and
chill. The flavours of the cheese
improve if it is made 1 or 2 days in
advance. Allow the cheese to come to
room temperature before serving.
Accompany with Melba toast or
biscuits (crackers). *Serves 6 to 8.*

— RICOTTA CHEESE BALLS —

1 kg (2 lb) Ricotta cheese
1 red pepper (capsicum), finely chopped
4 tablespoons finely chopped mixed fresh herbs
4 tablespoons black or toasted sesame seeds
1 teaspoon salt

Keep the Ricotta cheese well chilled. Form into 24 balls with a small ice cream scoop or a spoon. Divide the Ricotta balls into three groups. Roll the first group in the finely chopped red pepper. Place on a foil-lined tray and chill.

Roll the next group of balls in the chopped herbs. Some chopped spring onion may be added for more flavour.

Mix the black sesame seeds (available from Asian food shops) with the salt and roll the last balls in this. Chill all the Ricotta balls. To serve, arrange rows of the colourful balls on a platter. *Makes 24.*

– MORTADELLA TRIANGLES –

125 g (4 oz) Ricotta cheese
1 teaspoon horseradish sauce
2 tablespoons snipped fresh chives
salt and pepper
2 or 3 dill pickles or gherkins
3 slices mortadella

Mix the Ricotta cheese with the horseradish and chives, seasoning with salt and pepper to taste. Cut the dill pickles into thin slices.

Take one slice of mortadella, spread with half the cheese mixture and top with half the dill pickles. Add another layer of mortadella, spread remaining cheese over and top with the remaining dill pickles. Place the third slice of mortadella on top.

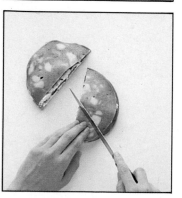

Store in the refrigerator in cling film (plastic wrap) until firm. Cut into 8 wedges just before serving. The triangles can be made 1 day in advance and kept chilled. *Makes 8.*

— RICOTTA CHEESE PUFFS —

250 g (8 oz) Ricotta cheese
2 eggs
2 tablespoons plain flour
1 teaspoon salt
3 spring onions, chopped
4 tablespoons chopped fresh parsley
2 teaspoons drained capers
vegetable oil for deep-frying

Place the cheese in a bowl and mix with a fork.

Add the eggs, flour, salt, onions, parsley and the capers. Stir with a fork until well mixed. If preparing in advance, cover and refrigerate.

Heat the oil and drop rounded teaspoonfuls of the Ricotta mixture into the oil, cooking only a few at a time. When golden all over, remove and drain. Cook the remaining mixture. Serve hot. *Makes about 20.*

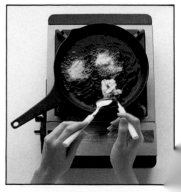

ROQUEFORT CHEESE SPREAD

125 g (4 oz) Roquefort or other blue cheese
125 g (4 oz) full fat soft (cream) cheese
1 tablespoon kirsch or port
60 g (2 oz) pecan nuts, coarsely chopped
whole pecans, to garnish

Beat the Roquefort cheese in a bowl with a fork until smooth. Add the cheese and kirsch and mix together until smooth. Stir the chopped nuts into the mixture.

Turn cheese mixture out on to a sheet of foil and shape into a single round or two small rounds. If mixture is very soft, chill until firm enough to handle.

Arrange the whole nuts around the cheese and place one nut on top. Chill until firm. Serve the cheese with pear and apple slices or biscuits (crackers). *Serves 8 to 10.*

ROQUEFORT BISCUITS

125 g (4 oz/1 cup) self-raising flour
125 g (4 oz) butter
60 g (2 oz) Roquefort or other blue cheese
60 g (2 oz) mature Cheddar cheese
75 g (2½ oz/½ cup) sesame seeds

Sift flour into a bowl and add the butter. Crumble in the Roquefort. Grate the Cheddar cheese and add. Mix all ingredients in the bowl together well using your fingers to form a dough. Chill.

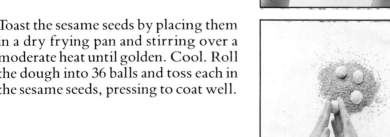

Toast the sesame seeds by placing them in a dry frying pan and stirring over a moderate heat until golden. Cool. Roll the dough into 36 balls and toss each in the sesame seeds, pressing to coat well.

Place the balls on greased baking trays and press out lightly with a fork. Bake at 200C (400F/Gas 6) for 10 minutes, or until the biscuits are golden around the edges. Cool on wire racks; store in an airtight container. *Makes 36.*

— DEEP-FRIED CAMEMBERT —

125 g (4 oz) round or semi-circle Camembert
  cheese, well chilled
1 egg, beaten
60 g (2 oz/½ cup) dry breadcrumbs
125 g (4 oz/¾ cup) sesame seeds
vegetable oil for deep-frying
fresh strawberries, to serve (optional)

Cut the Camembert into 6 wedges.

Dip the wedges of cheese, one at a
time, into the beaten egg, turning to
coat each wedge. Mix the breadcrumbs and sesame seeds together on a
sheet of greaseproof paper.

As each cheese wedge is coated with
egg, place in the sesame and
breadcrumb mixture, and coat the
cheese evenly. If not serving
immediately, put on a plate and chill.
Heat oil for deep-frying and fry the
cheese wedges a few at a time until
golden on all sides. Garnish with
strawberries and serve. *Makes 6
wedges.*

— SPINACH & FETA ROLLS —

2 tablespoons vegetable oil
2 onions, finely chopped
250 g (8 oz) packet frozen spinach, defrosted and
    drained
2 teaspoons dried dill
125 g (4 oz) feta cheese, crumbled
1 egg, beaten
3 tablespoons thick sour cream
12 sheets filo pastry
125 g (4 oz) butter, melted

Gently heat oil in a saucepan and sauté the onions until tender, but not coloured. Add the spinach and sauté for a further 2 minutes. Add the dill and feta cheese.

Remove from the heat and allow to cool. Mix in the egg and sour cream. Chill. Take 1 sheet of the filo pastry, (keep remaining sheets covered with damp absorbent paper) and brush with butter. Top with another sheet of filo and cut into 3 strips.

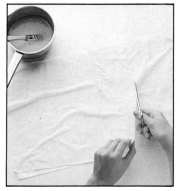

Spoon 1 tablespoon of the spinach mixture on one end of a strip and roll up, tucking in the edges. Brush the end with more butter to seal. Repeat with the remaining pastry and spinach filling. Place the rolls joined end down on baking trays and bake at 200C (400F/Gas 6) for about 15 minutes. Serve hot. *Makes 18.*

— EGG & CHIVE PINWHEELS —

1 loaf unsliced white bread
125 g (4 oz) butter, at room temperature
6 hard-boiled eggs
3 tablespoons mayonnaise
1 teaspoon hot English mustard
salt and pepper, to taste
6 tablespoons snipped fresh chives

Using an electric or serrated edged knife, cut the bread lengthwise into 5 slices. Cut away the crusts. Spread each slice with the butter.

Shell the eggs and mash with the mayonnaise and mustard. Season to taste with salt and pepper. Spread evenly on the slices of bread, almost to the edges. Sprinkle the chives over.

Roll up each slice of bread. Chill in cling film (plastic wrap) until ready to serve. Using a serrated or electric knife, cut each roll into 5 or 6 slices. Arrange on a platter. *Makes 25 to 30.*

EGG TAPENADE

6 hard–boiled eggs
18 black olives
5 canned anchovy fillets, drained
1 tablespoon drained capers
100 g (3½ oz) canned tuna, drained
3 tablespoons olive oil
lemon juice, to taste
fresh parsley leaves, to garnish

Shell the eggs and halve crosswise using a stainless steel knife. Remove the yolks and trim bases so eggs stand upright.

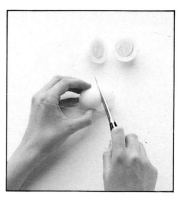

Reserve 6 olives for garnish. Cut the flesh away from the remaining olives and discard the stones. Put the olive flesh, anchovies, capers, egg yolks and drained tuna into the bowl of a food processor. Blend together, gradually adding the oil to make a thick purée. Season with lemon juice. Chill.

Spoon egg yolk mixture into the white halves. Slice reserved olives in half and place a slice on top of each egg. Garnish with parsley leaves. The eggs can be hard–boiled and prepared up to 2 days before serving. Keep whites in a bowl, with water to cover and refrigerate. *Makes 12.*

DEVILLED EGGS

12 eggs
1 teaspoon prepared English mustard
6 tablespoons mayonnaise
few drops of Tabasco sauce
pinch of cayenne pepper
2 teaspoons paprika
rolled anchovy fillets, to garnish
salt

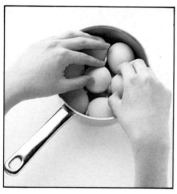

To boil eggs so the yolks are centred, tightly pack into a saucepan, pointed end down. Add water to cover, bring to the boil and cook for 10 minutes. Cook in 1 or 2 batches.

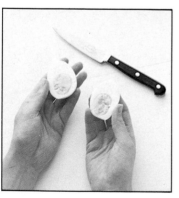

Drain the eggs and place under cold running water until they are cool. (Quick cooling prevents a black ring forming around the yolk.) Shell and halve the eggs using a stainless steel or silver knife (carbon steel will leave a black mark on the whites). Mash the yolks with the remaining ingredients, except anchovies, and season to taste with salt. Put into a piping bag.

If preparing ahead, store the yolk filling in the piping bag and the whites in a bowl of water to cover in the refrigerator. Drain the whites. Pipe the filling into the whites and decorate the top of each with an anchovy fillet. *Makes 24.*

EGG & SESAME ROLLS

3 eggs
salt
1 tablespoon water
2 tablespoons sesame seeds
2 teaspoons soy sauce
¼ teaspoon sugar
½ small onion, finely chopped
250 g (8 oz) packet frozen spinach, defrosted and
  drained
1 thick slice cooked ham, cut into 3 strips

Lightly beat eggs with ¼ teaspoon salt and water. Make 3 thin omelettes. Stir sesame seeds in a dry pan over a low heat until golden, then grind while hot. Gently cook onion in a little oil, add drained spinach and season with salt to taste. Cool.

Place 1 omelette on a Japanese bamboo mat, rounded side up, and spread one-third of the spinach mixture on one end, taking care not to spread right to the sides. Sprinkle with one-third of the sesame mixture and place a strip of ham down the centre.

Lift the mat so the omelette forms a roll, then roll again in the mat and press firmly. Leave for a few minutes, then unroll mat and cut the omelette roll into pieces. If liked, sprinkle with extra sesame seeds before serving. *Makes about 18.*

- EGG - RICOTTA TRIANGLES -

5 eggs
salt
1 tablespoon water
180 g (6 oz) Ricotta cheese
3 spring onions, chopped
4 tablespoons chopped fresh parsley
2 teaspoons chopped drained capers
½ red pepper (capsicum), cut into thin strips

Beat 3 of the eggs with a good pinch of salt and the water. Heat a greased 15 cm (6 in) frying pan and make 3 thin omelettes with the egg mixture.

Combine the cheese with remaining eggs, 1 teaspoon salt, the pepper, spring onions, parsley and capers. Place an omelette on a small plate and spread with a third of the cheese mixture. Add strips of red pepper. Repeat until all are used.

Place each plate in a steaming basket. Make sure the plate is small enough for the steam to circulate. Cover and steam for 15 minutes. Cut into small wedges, and serve either warm or chilled. *Makes about 9 wedges*.

—— EGG & CAVIAR SPREAD ——

4 eggs
60 g (2 oz) butter
salt and pepper
4 tablespoons thick sour cream
½ small onion, or 4 spring onions, finely chopped
3 tablespoons black caviar
biscuits (crackers), to serve
spring onion strips, to garnish

Put the eggs into a saucepan of cold water. Bring to the boil and cook for 10 minutes. Cool under running water and remove shells when cool enough to handle.

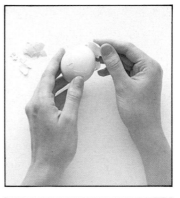

Mash the eggs finely using a potato masher. Melt the butter and pour, while hot, on to the warm eggs. Season with salt and pepper. Pack the egg mixture into a serving dish and chill. This can be prepared 1 day in advance.

Combine the sour cream with the onion. Just before serving, spread sour cream mixture over the egg. Top with the black caviar and spring onion strips. Serve with biscuits (crackers). *Serves 6 to 8.*

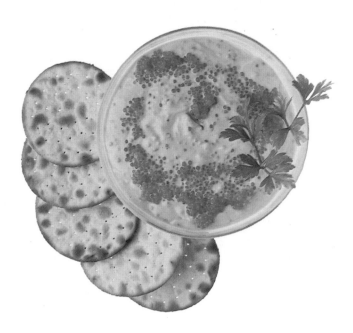

QUICK DIPS

CREAMY CORN DIP

300 g (10 oz), jar corn relish
300 ml (10 fl oz) carton thick sour cream
biscuits (crackers) or corn chips, to serve

Mix the jar of corn relish with the sour cream. Pile into a serving bowl and surround with biscuits or corn chips. *Serves 6 to 8.*

CAVIAR DIP

300 ml (10 fl oz) carton thick sour cream
50 g (1½ oz) jar red caviar
1 tablespoon finely chopped onion
fresh parsley sprig, to garnish
vegetable and biscuits (crackers), to serve

Mix the sour cream with half the caviar and the onion. Turn into a serving bowl and swirl in the rest of the caviar. Garnish with a parsley sprig and serve with vegetables or biscuits for dipping. *Serves 6 to 8.*

ANCHOVY DIP

300 ml (10 fl oz) carton thick sour cream
45 g (1½ oz) can anchovy fillets, drained and
    mashed
3 tablespoons chopped dill pickles
2 teaspoons drained capers
biscuits (crackers), to serve

Blend sour cream, anchovies and pickles. Turn into a bowl and garnish with the capers. Serve with biscuits. *Serves 6 to 8.*

AIOLI & CRUDITÉS

4 cloves garlic
½ teaspoon salt
2 egg yolks
250 ml (8 fl oz/1 cup) virgin olive oil
juice of ½ lemon
crisp vegetables, such as carrots, celery and
radish, to serve

Crush the garlic into a bowl, add the salt and egg yolks. Whisk together well. Add 1 or 2 drops of oil and whisk.

Continue whisking the egg yolk mixture, gradually adding the oil until about 2 tablespoons of the oil has been added. Add the remaining oil in a fine stream, whisking all the time. If the mixture becomes too thick, add a little hot water. Add the lemon juice and season with more salt, if needed. Cover and refrigerate.

Peel carrot and cut into 10 cm (4 in) lengths. Cut celery the same size and trim stem and root from radishes. Pile around the Aioli on a large platter. The vegetables are dipped into the Aioli before eating. Other vegetables such as mange tout (snow peas), cucumber sticks, fresh cauliflower florets, blanched asparagus tips and spring onions go well. *Serves 6 to 8.*

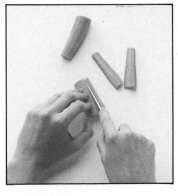

BAGNA CAUDA

2 or 3 carrots
½ cauliflower
other raw vegetables in season
45 g (1½ oz) canned anchovy fillets
125 g (4 oz) butter
125 ml (4 fl oz/½ cup) virgin olive oil or
**   vegetable oil**
4 cloves garlic, crushed
250 ml (8 fl oz/1 cup) double (thickened) cream
slices of crusty bread, to serve

Prepare the vegetables first: peel carrots and cut into 10 cm (4 in) length sticks; separate the cauliflower into florets and prepare other vegetables.

Drain the anchovies, chop and mash well. Melt the butter with the oil in a small pan and add the anchovies and garlic. Bring the mixture to a gentle boil, stirring all the time, and simmer for 5 minutes. Add the cream to the anchovy mixture. Heat gently, stirring while it thickens, for about 5 minutes. Do not boil.

Serve the anchovy sauce in a bowl while still hot. Provide wooden toothpicks for guests to spear their chosen vegetable, dip into the hot sauce and eat with a slice of crusty bread. *Serves 4 to 6.*

MEXICAN BEAN DIP

465 g (15 oz) canned red kidney beans
2 tablespoons vegetable oil
90 g (3 oz/¾ cup) grated Cheddar cheese
½ teaspoon salt
1 teaspoon chilli powder
1 tablespoon chopped green pepper (capsicum)
corn chips or prawn crisps for dipping

Drain the beans, reserving the liquid for the dip.

Heat the oil in a small pan and add the beans, mashing with a potato masher as they cook. Add 3 tablespoons of the reserved bean liquid and stir in until well mixed. Cool. Add cheese, salt and chilli powder. If the mixture is thick, add more of the reserved bean liquid until it is a good consistency for scooping. Add the pepper. Serve hot with corn chips or prawn crisps. *Serves 4 to 6.*

If using prawn crisps, drop a few at a time into deep hot oil. When they come to the top, remove almost immediately and drain. The crisps take only a few seconds to cook. Drain on absorbent paper and store in an airtight container until ready to use.

- PEANUT SAUCE & CRUDITÉS -

2 cloves garlic
2 tablespoons dark soy sauce
4 tablespoons smooth peanut butter
1 tablespoon sugar
250 ml (8 fl oz/1 cup) water
2 red chillies
selection of crisp vegetables, such as carrots, celery, a cucumber, radishes and a cauliflower

Crush the garlic and place in a small saucepan with the soy sauce, peanut butter, sugar and water.

Shred the chillies, removing the seeds. Put the chilli shreds into the pan and heat together. Simmer for 5 minutes, stirring constantly. If the mixture is very thin, simmer until it thickens slightly. Leave to cool. The sauce sometimes becomes solid when cool. When this happens thin with a little water. Pour into a serving bowl.

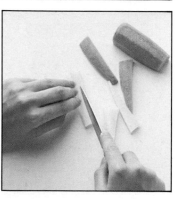

Prepare the vegetables for dipping. Cut carrots, celery and cucumber into 10 cm (4 in) fingers. Remove stems and roots from radishes. Break the cauliflower into florets — they may be blanched in boiling water if preferred. To serve, surround the bowl of dipping sauce with the vegetables. *Serves 4 to 6.*

GUACAMOLE

3 ripe avocados
1 clove garlic, crushed
1 teaspoon salt
1 small onion, finely chopped
few drops of Tabasco sauce
4 bacon rashers
corn chips, to serve

Halve 2 of the avocados, remove stones and scoop the flesh into a food processor or push through a sieve.

Add the garlic, salt, onion and Tabasco sauce and blend until smooth. Add more Tabasco sauce if a hot flavour is desired. Remove the rind from the bacon and grill until crisp. Cool.

Break the crisp bacon into small pieces and stir into the avocado purée. Cube the remaining avocado and stir into the purée. Serve with corn chips.
Serves 6 to 8.

Note: Guacamole is best made 1 to 2 hours before serving as the avocado tends to discolour. Keeping the mixture airtight and adding the stones from the avocado will help to prevent browning.

HUMMUS BI TAHINI

125 g (4 oz) chick-peas
salt
4 cloves garlic, crushed
125 g (4 oz/½ cup) tahini paste
juice of 2 lemons
1 tablespoon olive oil
paprika and fresh parsley sprig, to garnish
pitta bread, to serve

Wash the chick-peas and soak overnight in water to cover.

Drain chick-peas. Add fresh water to cover and 2 teaspoons salt. Cover and simmer for 2 hours or until tender. Purée the chick-peas in a food processor, adding a little of the cooking liquid to make a smooth paste. Add the crushed garlic, tahini paste and lemon juice to taste.

Turn into a serving bowl and smooth the surface. Drizzle olive oil over to prevent the hummus drying out and garnish with a pinch of paprika and a sprig of parsley. Serve with pitta bread. The bread may be split, torn into pieces and crisped in an oven at 150C (300F/Gas 2) for 10 to 15 minutes. This makes a good substitute for Melba toast. *Serves 12 to 15.*

—— MINTED SAMBAL DIP ——

4 spring onions
300 ml (10 fl oz) carton thick sour cream
1 teaspoon finely grated fresh root ginger
1 tablespoon lemon juice
1 tablespoon curry powder
6 - 8 tablespoons chopped fresh mint
1 clove garlic
1 teaspoon salt
fresh vegetables for dipping

Finely chop the spring onions including most of the green tops. Add to the sour cream with the ginger, lemon juice, curry powder and chopped mint. Mix well.

Peel garlic and crush the clove in salt until it forms a pulp. Add to the sour cream mixture and stir in well. If mixture is thin, whip until thickened. The flavour will improve if dip is chilled for at least 24 hours.

Select crisp fresh vegetables for the crudités. Peel and cut into 10 cm (4 in) lengths. Serve chilled with the dip. Suitable crudités are carrots and celery sticks, mange tout (snow peas), radishes, spring onions, blanched broccoli and cauliflower florets.
Serves 6 to 8.

SKEWERED BITES

PARMA HAM (PROSCIUTTO) AND MELON

1 small cantaloupe (rock) melon
250 g (8 oz) very thinly sliced Parma ham (prosciutto)

Peel the melon, cut into halves and scoop out the seeds. Cut the flesh into cubes. Take a ham slice, gather up and skewer on to a melon cube with a wooden toothpick. Serve chilled. *Makes about 48.*

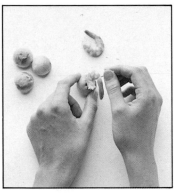

AVOCADO AND PRAWN

1 ripe avocado pear
500 g (1 lb) cooked prawns
juice of 1 lemon

Halve the avocado and remove the stone. Either scoop out the flesh with a melon baller or cut into cubes. Peel the prawns and de-vein. Skewer a prawn and piece of avocado together. Squeeze lemon juice over. Serve immediately. *Makes about 18.*

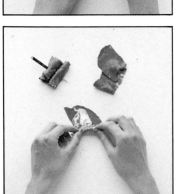

SMOKED BEEF ROLLS

2 tablespoons sour cream
1 teaspoon horseradish sauce
125 g (4 oz) thinly sliced smoked beef

Mix together sour cream and horseradish, spread on beef and roll up. Cut into 2.5 cm (1 in) pieces and serve 2 or 3 rolls on a toothpick. *Makes 8 to 10.*

— DEVILLED MIXED NUTS —

125 g (4 oz) almonds
45 g (1½ oz) butter
2 cloves garlic, crushed
1 teaspoon Worcestershire sauce
2 teaspoons curry powder
pinch of cayenne
125 g (4 oz) raw cashew nuts
125 g (4 oz) pecan nuts
chilli flower, to garnish (optional)

Blanch the almonds by pouring boiling water over the nuts and leaving a few minutes. Lift the nuts out and they will slip out of their skins easily.

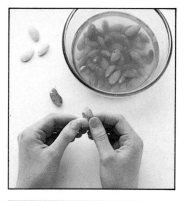

Melt the butter and stir in the garlic, Worcestershire sauce, curry powder and cayenne. Sprinkle evenly over all the nuts in an ovenproof dish and toss well to coat evenly with the spicy butter mixture.

Cook at 180C (350F/Gas 4) for 15 to 20 minutes, stirring every 5 minutes to colour evenly. Remove nuts from the oven and cool. Store in airtight container until ready to serve with drinks. Serve in a bowl and garnish with a chilli flower, if desired. *Serves 4 to 6.*

CRISPY WAFERS

MELINJO NUTS

These are the kernels of dried melinjo nuts which are flattened out into fine wafers. They are Indonesian in origin and are available from Asian food shops. Deep-fry them in hot vegetable oil until they puff up. Cook a few at a time and drain. Avoid browning them as this causes a bitter taste. Sprinkle with salt before serving.

PRAWN CRISPS

Available from Asian food shops, these wafers come in a dried form and are fried in deep vegetable oil until they puff and crisp. Cook a few at a time. They are available in many colours for attractive appearance, but generally the plain ones have a better flavour. They may be cooked ahead of time and stored in airtight containers.

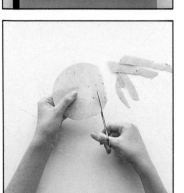

PAPPADOM STRIPS

With scissors, cut pappadoms into strips about the width of a finger. Heat a saucepan of deep vegetable oil and drop in the pappadom strips, a few at a time, until golden and crisp. Drain and serve with drinks. If liked the strips can be dusted with paprika mixed with a pinch of cayenne while still hot.

— SPICED CRACKED OLIVES —

1 kg (2 lb) large green olives
2 or 3 red chillies
4 cloves garlic, peeled
3 sprigs each fresh dill, thyme and oregano
2 teaspoons fennel seeds
olive oil, to cover

Make a lengthwise slit in each olive, cutting in as far as the stone. (This allows flavours to penetrate.)

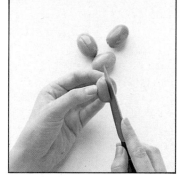

Put olives into a jar with the chillies, garlic, dill, thyme, oregano and fennel seeds. Pour in oil to cover and store, covered in the refrigerator for several days or weeks. Drain and serve as an appetizer with drinks or in salads. More olives can be added to the oil, or the oil may be used afterwards for cooking or in salads. *Makes 1 kg (2 lb).*

CALAMATTA OLIVES WITH GARLIC

Put calamatta olives (a variety of Greek olive with distinctive flavour), with peeled cloves of garlic in a jar and pour in olive oil or a mixture of olive and vegetable oil. Cover and store in the refrigerator for a few days or several weeks. Drain and serve. The oil may be used for cooking and salad dressings. A few whole chillies may be added to give bite.

— PICKLED VEGETABLES —

250 g (8 oz) cauliflower
250 g (8 oz) carrots
1 red pepper (capsicum)
250 ml (8 fl oz/1 cup) white distilled vinegar
60 g (2 oz/¼ cup) sugar
1 teaspoon salt
1 teaspoon mustard seeds
1 teaspoon black peppercorns
125 g (4 oz) mange tout (snow peas)

Cut the cauliflower into florets. Peel carrots and cut into 10 cm (4 in) lengths. Cut the pepper and carrots into 10 cm (4 in) lengths.

Drop the cauliflower, carrots and pepper into a saucepan of boiling water. Return to the boil, then drain vegetables immediately and rinse under cold water.

Stir together the vinegar, sugar, salt, mustard seeds and peppercorns until the sugar dissolves. Add the boiled vegetables. Cover and chill for 2 days, turning vegetables occasionally for the pickle flavours to penetrate. String the mange tout and add 2 hours before serving. Serve chilled, either plain or with a dipping sauce. *Serves 6 to 8.*

EGG & NORI ROLLS

3 eggs
salt
1 tablespoon cold water
2 sheets nori (sheets dried laver seaweed available from Asian food shops)

Beat the eggs with salt to taste and water until mixed. Set aside. Toast the sheets of nori by holding briefly over a gas flame. The nori may be also toasted by quickly running it across an electric hotplate set at a moderate heat. Take care not to burn the nori.

Reserve 1 teaspoonful of the egg mixture. Make 4 thin omelettes with the remaining egg mixture in a greased frying pan, cooking on one side only.

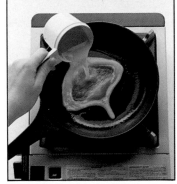

Place one omelette, uncooked side up, on a bamboo mat, top with the nori, trimmed to size, then another omelette until all are used. Roll up the omelettes in the mat and seal the edge with the reserved egg. Make a tight, compact roll and leave until cold. Remove the mat and cut into rolls. *Makes 6 to 8.*

STUFFED FRUIT

PRUNES WITH WALNUT FILLING

12 prunes
60 g (2 oz) full fat soft (cream) cheese
1 tablespoon chopped walnuts
12 walnuts halves

Remove stones from the prunes. Soften the cheese and beat in the nuts. Stuff the prunes with the cheese mixture and top each with a walnut half. Chill before serving. *Makes 12.*

FIGS WITH CAMEMBERT

250 g (8 oz) dried figs
3 tablespoons port
125 g (4 oz) round or semi-circle Camembert
    cheese, diced

Soak the figs in the port for several hours. Cut a slit in the fig and form a hole with your finger. Fill with the cheese. *Makes about 15.*

FRESH DATES WITH GINGER

250 g (8 oz) fresh dates
125 g (4 oz) full fat soft (cream) cheese
1 tablespoon chopped glacé ginger
1 teaspoon grated lemon rind

Remove stones from dates. Beat the cheese with the ginger and lemon rind. Fill the dates with the mixture. *Makes about 15.*

POOR MAN'S CAVIAR

2 aubergines (eggplants)
salt and pepper
4 tablespoons olive oil
1 clove garlic, crushed
2 canned anchovy fillets, drained (optional)
2 tablespoons white vinegar
1 tablespoon lemon juice

Halve the aubergines and score the flesh deeply in a diamond pattern. Sprinkle the aubergines liberally with salt and place upside down in one layer in a dish and leave for at least 1 hour.

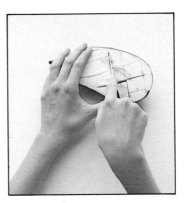

Drain the juices from the aubergines, rinse under cold running water and drain well. Place on a baking tray, season with a good grinding of black pepper and drizzle 2 tablespoons of the oil over. Bake at 180C (350F/Gas 4) for 1 hour or until very soft. Cool slightly.

Scoop the flesh of the aubergines into the bowl of a food processor. Add the garlic and anchovies and blend until smooth. Gradually whisk in the remaining oil, drop by drop at first, then in a thin stream until the purée is thick. Add the vinegar and lemon juice to taste. Serve in a bowl surrounded with biscuits (crackers). *Serves 8 to 10.*

— MARINATED ARTICHOKES —

400 g (14 oz) can artichoke hearts
6 tablespoons olive or vegetable oil
pepper
3 tablespoons chopped fresh mixed herbs
salt
juice of ½ lemon
red chilli slivers (optional)
1 clove garlic, crushed (optional)

Drain the artichokes and rinse well under a cold running water to remove all the brine. Drain again and cut into halves or quarters.

Place the artichokes in a bowl, add the oil, a good grinding of pepper and the herbs. Mix together well, cover and refrigerate until ready to serve. Toss again before serving and add a squeeze of lemon juice and salt to taste.

For a bite, some slivers of fresh red chilli may be added to the artichokes; for garlic lovers, add a crushed garlic clove before chilling. The artichokes may be stored in a jar for up to 2 weeks, provided they are covered with the oil. Serve at room temperature. They may also be served on a croûton or added to salads. *Serves 4 to 6.*

ASPARAGUS ROLLS

25 spears fresh or canned asparagus
4 egg yolks
250 g (8 oz) butter
squeeze of lemon juice
1 tablespoon chopped fresh mint
1 loaf unsliced bread

If using fresh asparagus, trim the stalks and cook in a pan of boiling water for 8 minutes. Drain and rinse with cold water. If using canned asparagus, drain.

To make the Hollandaise sauce, whip the egg yolks in a food processor until frothy. Melt the butter. When very hot, gradually add to the yolks, in a thin stream, with the processor on all the time. Transfer to a bowl and chill the mixture until thickened. Flavour the Hollandaise with lemon juice to taste and stir in the mint.

Use a serrated or electric knife to cut the bread into 25 thin slices. Cut away the crusts. Spread bread slices with the Hollandaise sauce and place one asparagus spear, cut in half, on each piece. Join two corners of each with a wooden toothpick. Dot with more sauce. Place under a preheated grill and cook until crisp. *Makes 25.*

CRISP SPLIT PEAS

180 g (6 oz/1 cup) yellow split peas
2 teaspoons bicarbonate of soda
oil for deep-frying
½ teaspoon chilli powder
½ teaspoon ground coriander
pinch each ground cinnamon and cloves
1 teaspoon salt
chilli flower, to garnish (optional)

Wash the peas in cold water and drain. Cover with fresh cold water, add the bicarbonate of soda and soak over-night.

Rinse peas, wash again in fresh water and drain thoroughly. Leave for at least 30 minutes, then turn on to absorbent paper to dry. Heat about 5 cm (2 in) oil and deep-fry the peas, in several small batches, until they are golden. Take care when frying the peas – even when thoroughly dry they tend to cause the oil to bubble to the top of the pan. Remove from the hot oil with a slotted spoon and drain on absorbent paper.

Continue to cook the remaining peas in the same way, then turn them into a dish. Sprinkle the chilli powder, coriander, cinnamon, cloves and salt over the fried peas. Mix thoroughly so the peas are well coated. Cool and store in airtight containers. Serve in a bowl, garnished with a chilli flower if desired. *Serves 6 to 8.*

— CUCUMBER SANDWICHES —

2 cucumbers
3 teaspoons salt
1 loaf sliced white or brown bread
125 g (4 oz) butter
pepper
3 tablespoons thick sour cream
1 bunch snipped fresh chives

Thinly slice the cucumbers. (If using the tough-skinned variety, peel and remove seeds first.) Sprinkle with salt, put a plate and weight on top and leave for several hours.

Drain all the juices from the cucumbers, rinse under cold water to remove excess salt, drain and pat dry between sheets of absorbent paper. Chill until ready to use. Remove the crusts from the bread and butter the slices on one side only. Top half the slices with the cucumber and cover with the remaining slices of bread, buttered side down.

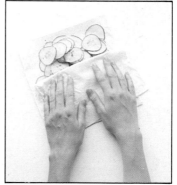

Cut each sandwich diagonally into quarters. Spread the sour cream on one of the cut sides of each triangle and dip into the snipped chives. Arrange on a platter. *Makes 48.*

CUCUMBER & SALMON ROLLS

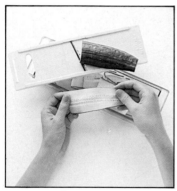

1 cucumber (use long ones with few seeds)
bottled horseradish sauce
10 thin slices of smoked salmon
strips of pickled ginger (available from Asian
food shops)

Cut the cucumbers into 12 cm (5 in) lengths and trim away the ends. Use a mandolin or Oriental vegetable slicer to cut the cucumber into thin lengthwise strips.

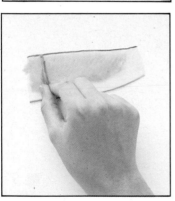

Spread each slice of cucumber with a smear of horseradish. Cut the smoked salmon slices the same width as the cucumber but only 7.5 cm (3 in) long. Place on the cucumber slices and put a few strips of the pickled ginger on one end of each slice.

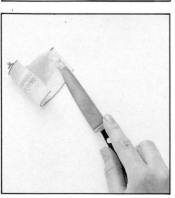

Roll up the cucumber slices, securing the ends by dabbing with a little horseradish so the coils adhere. Place on a platter with the red pickled ginger facing upwards. Serve immediately. *Makes about 20.*

– MARINATED MUSHROOMS –

500 g (1 lb) button mushrooms
250 ml (8 fl oz/1 cup) water
2 teaspoons salt
125 ml (4 fl oz/½ cup) white wine vinegar
1 bay leaf
few sprigs fresh thyme
1 clove garlic
2 tablespoons olive oil
1 lemon
finely chopped fresh parsley

Trim mushroom stalks. If necessary, wipe the mushrooms with a cloth dipped in water with a little lemon juice added.

Boil the water with the salt, vinegar, bay leaf, thyme, garlic and the oil. Put the mushrooms in a heatproof bowl and pour the boiling mixture over. When cool, refrigerate for at least 12 hours, or up to 3 days.

Drain the mushrooms and put in a serving bowl. Using a citrus zester, cut the lemon rind into fine strips and sprinkle over the mushrooms with the chopped parsley. *Serves 6 to 8.*

MUSHROOM PASTIES

125 g (4 oz/1 cup) plain flour
90 g (3 oz) butter
1 tablespoon water
3 spring onions, chopped
250 g (8 oz) button mushrooms, chopped
1 tablespoon plain flour
1 tablespoon dry sherry
¼ teaspoon dry mustard
2 tablespoons milk
8 olives, sliced
salt and pepper
1 egg beaten, to glaze

Sift flour into a bowl and rub in 60 g (2 oz) butter. Add the water to make a firm dough. Wrap and chill.

Sauté the onions in the remaining butter in a frying pan, without browning. Add the mushrooms and cook, stirring, until all the liquid evaporates. Stir in the flour and mix well. Add the sherry, mustard and milk and stir until mixture boils. Add the olives and season to taste. Allow this mushroom filling to cool.

Thinly roll out the pastry on a floured surface and cut into 7.5 cm (3 in) rounds. Brush edges with egg. Put a good teaspoonful of the filling in the centre of each round. Bring up the edges to join and pinch together. Place on greased baking trays, brush with egg to glaze and bake at 200C (400F/Gas 6) for 15 to 20 minutes. *Makes 10.*

AVOCADO MOUSSE

3 avocados
2 tablespoons lemon juice
2 teaspoons salt
2 tablespoons gelatine
250 ml (8 fl oz/1 cup) boiling water
1 tablespoon single cream
chopped red pepper (capsicum) and fresh parsley leaves, to garnish

Halve two of the avocados, remove stones and scoop the pulp into the bowl of a food processor. Add lemon the juice and salt.

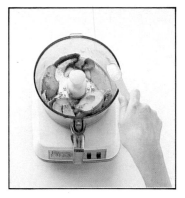

Dissolve gelatine in the boiling water and add to the avocado in the food processor. Mix together until smooth, then blend in the cream. Pour into individual moulds which have been rinsed in cold water. Chill until set.

Dip the moulds quickly into hot water and turn out mousses on to a platter, easing with a knife if necessary. Thinly slice the flesh of the third avocado. Garnish mousse with slices of avocado, pepper and parsley. Serve with biscuits (crackers).

Note: To make a loaf prepare a glaze by dissolving 1 tablespoon gelatine in 250 ml (8 fl oz/1 cup) boiling chicken stock. Pour half into a loaf tin. When set, top with the garnish and pour over the remaining glaze. When set add the avocado mousse. Chill and turn out as above. *Serves 8 to 10.*

PISSALADIÈRE

3 sheets puff pastry or 1½/350 g (12 oz) packets frozen puff pastry, defrosted
3 or 4 tomatoes
pepper
6 - 8 calamatta olives
1 egg, beaten, to glaze
45 g (1½ oz) canned anchovy fillets

Cut each sheet of pastry into two 12 x 15 cm (5 x 6 in) rectangles. Place on greased baking trays. If using block pastry, roll out thinly and cut into rectangles. Cut the trimmings into 1½ cm (½ in) strips and place along edges of the pastry squares to form borders.

Prick the centre of the pastry with a fork. Halve the tomatoes and cut into slices. Arrange slices, overlapping, in rows on the pastry. Generously grind pepper over the top.

Cut the olive flesh away from the stones and place on the tomatoes. Drain the anchovies and arrange the strips on top. Brush the borders of the pastries with beaten egg and bake at 200C (400F/Gas 6) for 5 minutes, until golden. Serve warm, cutting each rectangle into quarters. *Makes 24 wedges.*

MINI PIZZAS

15 g (½ oz) fresh (compressed) yeast
1 teaspoon sugar
250 ml (8 fl oz/1 cup) lukewarm water
300 g (10 oz/2½ cups) plain flour
½ teaspoon salt
2 onions, chopped
2 cloves garlic, crushed
2 tablespoons oil
4 to 6 tomatoes, skinned and sliced
2 teaspoons tomato paste
salt and pepper
125 g (4 oz) sliced spicy Italian salami
125 g (4 oz) mozzarella cheese
20 black olives

Cream the yeast with the sugar until it forms a liquid. Mix in the water.

Add yeast mixture to the flour and salt in a large bowl and form a dough. Knead for at least 5 minutes on a well floured surface. Turn into a greased bowl, cover and leave in a warm place about 1 hour, until double in bulk. Meanwhile, gently sauté the onion and garlic in oil for 2 minutes. Add the tomatoes and simmer until the sauce thickens, about 20 minutes. Stir in the tomato paste and season. Cut salami into quarters, the cheese into small pieces and the olives into chunks.

Turn the dough on to a board, knead lightly and roll out until 1 cm (½ in) thick. Cut into rounds with a 7.5 cm (3 in) cutter. Place on greased baking trays and top with sauce, then salami, cheese and olives. Bake at 200C (400F/ Gas 6) for 20 to 30 minutes. *Makes about 12.*

SUSHI IN SEAWEED

1 quantity sushi rice, page 22
6 sheets nori (dried laver seaweed)
6 dried Chinese mushrooms
2 tablespoons soy sauce
2 teaspoons sugar
1 cucumber
2 carrots

Prepare the rice as described. Toast a sheet of seaweed by holding over a gas flame or passing directly over an electric hotplate a few times. Place on a bamboo mat. Spread one-sixth of the rice over two-thirds of the seaweed.

Soak the mushrooms in boiling water for 20 minutes. Drain, discard the stacks and slice the caps. Simmer caps with soy and sugar until the liquid evaporates. Cut the cucumber and carrot into thin pencil-like lengths and arrange in a line down one edge of the rice. Top with a layer of the Chinese mushrooms.

Roll the sushi on the mat, keeping a firm pressure on the rice and lifting the mat so it forms a neat cylinder. Then roll the cylinder tightly in the mat. Leave for 10 minutes, unroll and cut each roll into 6 pieces. Repeat with remaining rice and seaweed. Serve cold. *Makes 36 pieces.*

— GINGERED FRUIT KEBABS —

**1 cantaloupe (rock) melon or honeydew melon
(or a mixture of both)
125 g (4 oz) strawberries
300 ml (10 fl oz) carton thick sour cream or
natural yogurt
1 tablespoon honey
1 tablespoon chopped glacé ginger
1 tablespoon chopped mint**

Select a variety of fruit in season, such as pineapples, apples, pears, or citrus fruit. Peel where necessary and cut the fruit into bite size pieces.

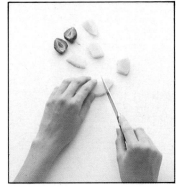

Thread the fruit on to bamboo skewers, alternating the different fruits. If preparing ahead, lay the skewered fruit in a container, cover and chill until ready to serve.

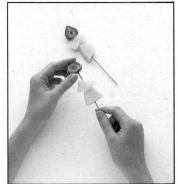

To make the honey sauce, combine the sour cream, honey, ginger and mint. Chill until ready to serve. Turn dipping sauce into a bowl and surround with kebabs. *Makes about 20.*

—— LAMB TRIANGLES ——

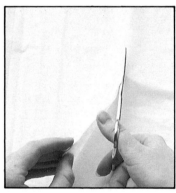

1 clove garlic, crushed
1 teaspoon grated fresh root ginger
1 onion, finely chopped
1 tablespoon oil
1 tablespoon curry powder
1 tablespoon white distilled vinegar
250 g (8 oz) lean minced cooked lamb
125ml (4 fl oz/½ cup) water
2 tablespoons chopped mint
salt
1 egg, beaten
3 sheets filo pastry
melted butter, to glaze

Cook garlic, ginger and onion in oil for 1 minute. Add curry powder and stir for another minute. Add vinegar, lamb and water and simmer for 5 minutes. Add mint and season to taste. Mix in egg, then cool. Cut pastry into 5 cm (2 in) wide strips. Keep pastry covered with a damp cloth to prevent drying out.

Layer two strips of pastry and brush with melted butter. Put a spoonful of filling in 1 corner and fold the pastry over the filling.

Continue to fold pastry over, keeping the triangular shape. Brush top with melted butter and place on buttered baking trays. Repeat until all are made. Bake at 200C (400F/Gas 6) for 20 minutes or until golden and crisp. Cool slightly before serving. *Makes 24.*

DOLMADES

180 g (6 oz) packet vine leaves
1 onion, finely chopped
2 tablespoons olive oil
500 g (16 oz/2 cups) cooked rice
salt and pepper
2 tablespoons chopped fresh mint
90 g (3 oz/1 cup) toasted pine nuts

Drain the vine leaves, rinse well and soak in cold water to remove the brine, separating the leaves carefully. Drain.

Gently sauté the onion in the oil. When tender, add to the rice and season to taste with salt and pepper. Stir in the mint and half the nuts. Place 2 teaspoons of this filling on each vine leaf, roll up and tuck in the edges.

Pack stuffed vine leaves close together in a shallow pan, making more than 1 layer if necessary, and separating the layers with extra vine leaves. Add enough hot water barely to cover the vine leaves. Place a plate directly on top of the rolls with a can on top to weigh them down. Cover and simmer for 30 minutes. Cool, then chill. Serve garnished with remaining pine nuts. *Makes about 45.*

Clockwise from top: Spicy Pork Rolls, page 45; Almond–Cheese
Balls, page 72; Chicken Satay, page 55

Avocado Mousse, page 115

Clockwise from top: Chinese Dumplings, page 44; Chicken and
Leek Rolls, page 58; Spring Rolls, page 43

Sushi With Prawns, page 22; Sushi In Seaweed, page 118

Clockwise from top: Cucumber & Salmon Rolls, page 112; Sage & Onion Pinwheels, page 76; Egg Tapenade, page 87; Spiced Cracked Olives, page 103

Salmon & Avocado Mousse, glazed and decorated, page 28

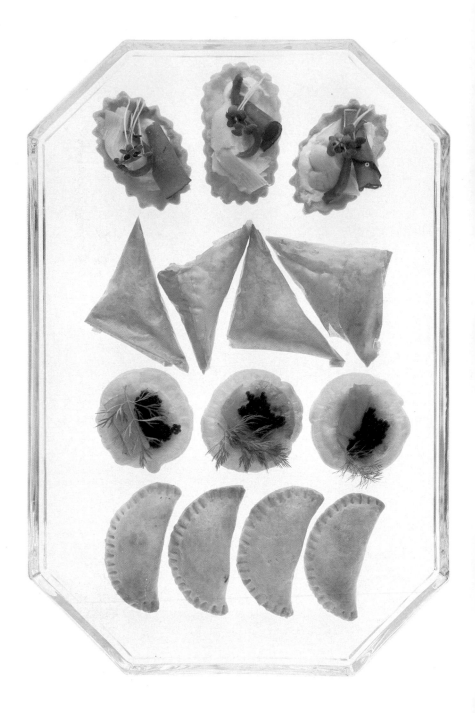

Top to bottom: Smoked Beef Tarts, page 61; Lamb Triangles, page 120; Smoked Salmon Quiches, page 30; Ham Crescents, page 39

Caviar Mousse, page 14

INDEX